The American Civil War, 1861–1865

REID MITCHELL

Longman

An imprint of **Pearson Education**

Harlow, England · London · New York · Reading, Massachusetts · San Francisco · Toronto · Don Mills, Ontario · Sydney
Tokyo · Singapore · Hong Kong · Seoul · Taipei · Cape Town · Madrid · Mexico City · Amsterdam · Munich · Paris · Milan

Pearson Education Limited
Edinburgh Gate
Harlow
Essex CM20 2JE
England
and Associated Companies throughout the world.

Visit us on the World Wide Web at:
www.pearsoneduc.com

First published 2001

ISBN 0-582-31973-0 PPR

British Library Cataloguing-in-Publication Data
A catalogue record for this book is
available from the British Library

Library of Congress Cataloging-in-Publication Data
Mitchell, Reid.
    The American Civil War, 1861-1865 / Reid Mitchell.
        p. cm. -- (Seminar studies in history)
    Includes bibliographical references and index.
    ISBN 0-582-31973-0 (pbk.)
        1. United States--History--Civil War, 1861-1865. Title. II. Series.

E468 .M56 2000
973.7--dc21   00-052010

Set by 7 in 10/12 Sabon Roman
Printed in Malaysia , LSP

'The youngest of us are never again to see the republic in which we were born.'

Wendell Phillips, 1864

CONTENTS

INTRODUCTION TO THE SERIES

Such is the pace of historical enquiry in the modern world that there is an ever-widening gap between the specialist article or monograph, incorporating the results of current research, and general surveys, which inevitably become out of date. *Seminar Studies in History* is designed to bridge this gap. The series was founded by Patrick Richardson in 1966 and his aim was to cover major themes in British, European and world history. Between 1980 and 1996 Roger Lockyer continued his work, before handing the editorship over to Clive Emsley and Gordon Martel. Clive Emsley is Professor of History at the Open University, while Gordon Martel is Professor of International History at the University of Northern British Columbia, Canada, and Senior Research Fellow at De Montfort University.

All the books are written by experts in their field who are not only familiar with the latest research but have often contributed to it. They are frequently revised, in order to take account of new information and interpretations. They provide a selection of documents to illustrate major themes and provoke discussion, and also a guide to further reading. The aim of *Seminar Studies in History* is to clarify complex issues without over-simplifying them, and to stimulate readers into deepening their knowledge and understanding of major themes and topics.

NOTE ON REFERENCING SYSTEM

Readers should note that numbers in square brackets [5] refer them to the corresponding entry in the Bibliography at the end of the book (specific page numbers are given in italics). A number in square brackets preceded by *Doc.* [*Doc. 5*] refers readers to the corresponding item in the Documents section which follows the main text.

ACKNOWLEDGEMENTS

The publishers are grateful to the US Library of Congress for permission to reproduce the images in the plate section.

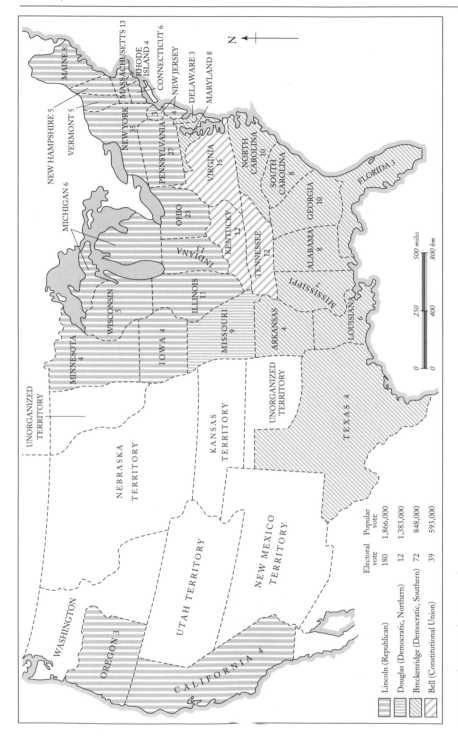

Map 1   The 1860 election results

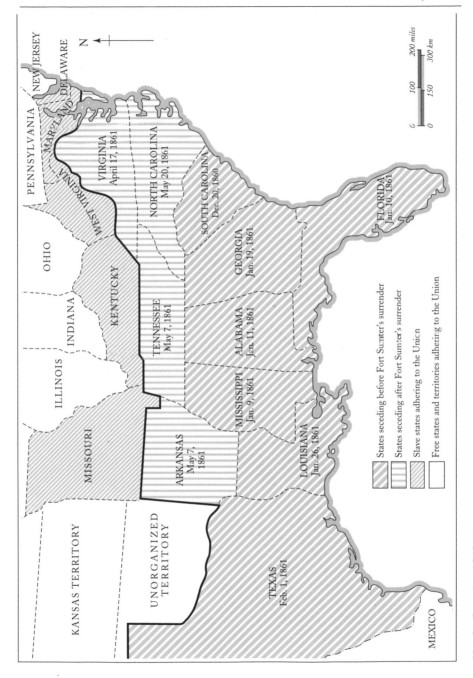

Map 2   Secession, 1860–61

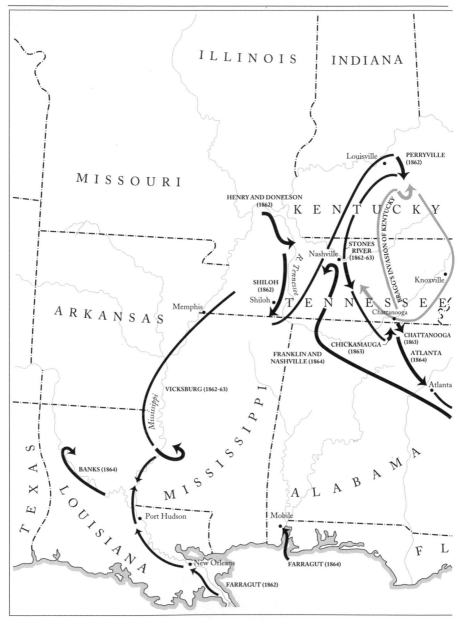

Map 3   The principle campaigns of the American Civil War

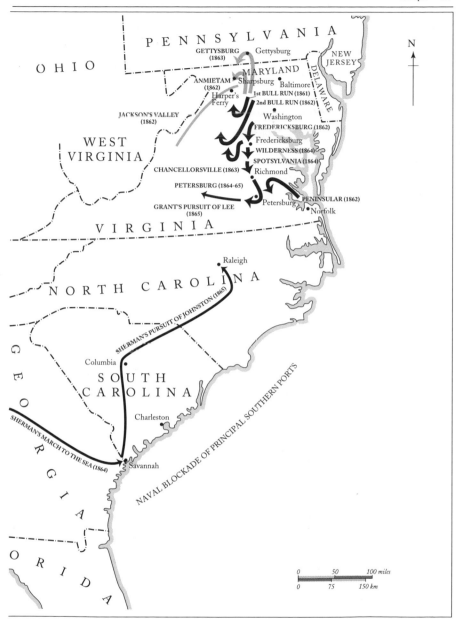

Map 4   The position of major Union and Confederate forces, 1 June 1863

PENNSYLVANIA

●Gettysburg

NEW
JERSEY

●Columbus

OHIO

Baltimore

DELAWARE

Harper's Ferry

Winchester●

●Washington

●Charleston

WEST
VIRGINIA

Fredericksburg

Richmond

Petersburg

Norfolk

VIRGINIA

NORTH CAROLINA

SOUTH
CAROLINA

Wilmington

G
E
O
R
G
I
A

Charleston

Savannah

⬜ Active armies

◯ Positions being held

— Union forces

— Confederate forces

F
L
O
R
I
D
A

N

| 0 | 50 | 100 miles |
| 0 | 75 | 150 km |

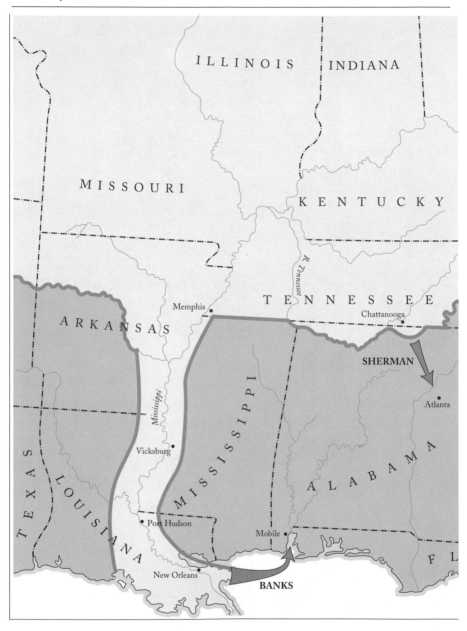

Map 5   Grant's plan for the 1864 campaign

PENNSYLVANIA

NEW JERSEY

OHIO

Harper's Ferry

Washington

MEADE

DELAWARE

SIGEL

Fredericksburg

WEST VIRGINIA

Richmond

Petersburg

BUTLER

Norfolk

VIRGINIA

NORTH CAROLINA

Raleigh

SOUTH CAROLINA

Wilmington

GEORGIA

Charleston

Savannah

FLORIDA

N

☐ Area under Federal Control

▨ Area under Confederate Control

0   50   100 miles

0   75   150 km

PART ONE   BACKGROUND

INTRODUCTION: THE PROBLEM

In 1861, former United States Army officer William Tecumseh Sherman lived in Pineville, Louisiana, where he worked as the head of the newly-established Louisiana Seminary of Learning and Military Academy. Following the election of Abraham Lincoln to the presidency and the secession of South Carolina, Louisiana seceded from the Union, joined the new Confederacy, and seized federal arsenals within the state. When war between the Confederacy and the Union appeared inevitable, the Louisiana Seminary broke up. The students and faculty would join the Confederate army; Sherman would return to the North and fight for the Union. In a last meeting with a fellow professor, Sherman warned him that southerners had no idea what they were doing, that no agricultural people could defeat a mechanized people, and that the North would fight in earnest. When it was time, however, for Sherman to make his formal farewell to the students and faculty, he discovered himself unable to speak. All he could do was touch his hand to his heart and say, 'You are here.'

* * *

Civil War historians have the habit of pointing to the war's death toll as a sign of its importance. The figures are daunting – an estimated 620,000 dead, almost as many American dead as in all other wars put together. (There is a kind of deceit built into these figures, as Americans fought on both sides of the Civil War; still, the estimated 320,000 Union dead would be impressive enough on their own.) Almost one in five white male southerners of military age died in the war; northern deaths – an estimated six percent – were a far lower proportion but still the highest percentage of deaths the United States has suffered in a war. Furthermore, about 275,000 soldiers on each side were maimed.

Lest this grisly catalogue somehow continue the romanticization of the war, we should remember that disease killed about two-thirds of these men. Diarrhea and dysentery – which is diarrhea with the presence of blood in the stool – killed as many soldiers as all the gunshots, saber-cuts, and cannon fire combined. The soldier of the era was less likely to die in a spectacular charge than lying in his own filth until dehydration put an end to him.

Sometimes the consequences of a war do come largely from its carnage and attendant horrors; one thinks of the First World War. But very few historians have considered the impact that all those deaths had on the Civil War generation. Its importance is more often summarized by its results: the preservation of the Union and the end of slavery. Emancipation was the single most revolutionary event in American history. Unfortunately, the war failed to resolve another fundamental issue for the United States: the question of race, racial conflict, and the institutions and culture of white supremacy.

Historians, however, have been too eager to attribute more to the Civil War than even it merits. Changes in governmental structure, economic development, the status of women and minorities, American ideas and literature, and many more have been credited to the war. In his masterful *The North Fights the Civil War: The Home Front*, however, J. Matthew Gallman finds more continuity than change in the North. Even in the revolutionized South, historians have been able to trace significant continuities between the old order and the new.

How much of postwar American development to attribute to the war is one of the many questions fundamental to Civil War history. Other questions include the war's place in the history of warfare, why the Confederacy lost and the Union won, the unfolding of emancipation, what the war reveals about northern and southern society. The war was more than a matter of brave men killing other brave men – it involved the homefront, the economy, the political system, the Constitution, the diplomatic arena, it affected women as well as men. Many of the issues of the period – warfare and violence, the sovereignty of nations, and matters of race – are not safely in the past, to be taken down and admired and put back on the shelf where they can't hurt us. Finally, that which William Faulkner called the 'eternal verities of the human heart' were with us then as much as now.

The number of questions brought to the Civil War for answer seems endless. They are best summed up by the nonsensical, inevitable, heartfelt question that underlies most Civil War history: what did the Civil War mean? One should follow the poets perhaps, and announce 'a war doesn't mean, it is.' To look for the meaning of the Civil War is to return to providential history. Abraham Lincoln was only the best known American of the Civil War generation to encourage a providential explanation, and his Second Inaugural Address is its most famous statement.

> The Almighty has His own purposes. Woe unto the world because of offences, for it must needs be that offences come, but woe to that man by whom the offence cometh. If we shall suppose that American slavery is one

of these offences which, in the providence of God, must needs come, but which having continued through His appointed time, He now wills to remove, and that He gives to both North and South this terrible war as the woe due to those by whom the offence came, shall we discern there any departure from those Divine attributes which the believers in a living God always ascribe to Him? Fondly do we hope, fervently do we pray, that this mighty scourge of war may speedily pass away. Yet if God wills that it continue until all the wealth piled up by the bondsman's two hundred and fifty years of unrequited toil shall be sunk, and until every drop of blood drawn with the lash shall be paid by another drawn with the sword, as it was said three thousand years ago, so, still it must be said that the judgments of the Lord are true and righteous altogether.

Faced with the magnitude of the Civil War and its repercussions, it was impossible that Americans of the mid-nineteenth century would fail to look to God for its meaning. And even today some find only in the notion of providential history a cause commensurate with the consequences.

CHAPTER TWO

ORIGINS OF THE CIVIL WAR

SECESSION

If we choose, we can trace the origins of the secession crisis to one of the most famous years in colonial history, 1619. That was when a Dutch man-of-war sold '20 odd Negars' to the colony of Virginia, although we will never know if these Africans were enslaved for life or not. While choosing this year has the appropriate sweep for a crisis that was indeed predicated on so much of America's past, picking 1619 would be facile. That Dutch man-of-war has too often been portrayed as the serpent in the American Eden. It took several generations for slavery to become established in Virginia; given the strength of slavery in the Sugar Islands, it was unlikely that slavery would not spread to the mainland of British North America. Furthermore, all of the thirteen colonies that declared independence from Britain in 1776 recognized slavery. It would be surprising if they had not, since, as David Brian Davis has shown, slavery is so nearly ubiquitous throughout time that the real historical question is how antislavery and emancipation arose in the western world during the eighteenth century [6].

The American Revolution itself could be considered the best starting point for a study of the secession crisis. Confederates justified secession by the Constitution but they also claimed the right of revolution, whereupon Unionists argued that the United States, by winning the War for Independence, had created the states themselves. During the Revolutionary period the North began the process of gradual emancipation that led to the conflict between free-labor and slave-labor states. But the Revolutionary generation failed to commit the new United States to universal freedom; nor was the continued existence of slavery sufficient to prevent the union of all thirteen states. While Americans like to believe that the Revolution was somehow inherently antislavery, it led to the creation of the world's largest slaveholding republic. Furthermore, while most northerners and indeed many southerners of 1861 insisted that the Revolutionary War and the Constitution had created a 'perpetual Union,' Kenneth Stampp has shown that this belief originated not with the generation of 1776 but in the nineteenth century [32].

Southern secessionists and Unionists North and South had profoundly different ideas about the origins of the United States. Secessionists argued that the Constitution created the nation upon its ratification by the states that were party to it. It was a compact among the states and if some states failed to honor it, that failure relieved other states of its obligations. Unionists looked toward the Revolutionary War rather than the Constitution. Without the efforts of the Continental Congress and the Continental Army, there would have been no sovereign states to ratify the Constitution; the nation had created the states.

Perhaps the origins of the Civil War are best looked for in the nineteenth century, which witnessed the capitalist transformation of the United States, the growth of nationalism throughout the western world, and a new sense of religious commitment in many Americans. Certainly the newly invigorated antislavery movements came from the religious fervor of the early nineteenth century.

In the middle of the eighteenth century some Europeans and Americans began questioning the enslavement of Africans, challenging first the African slave trade and then the institution of slavery itself. Three strands of not-entirely compatible beliefs influenced this shift. Radical Christians, particularly Quakers and Methodists, saw slaveholding as sinful, a perpetual act of war. Enlightenment thinkers held that slavery conflicted with the natural rights of man. Finally, an emerging capitalist argument condemned slavery as inefficient.

Emancipation was an international movement. As Latin American countries gained independence from Spain, they freed their slaves. France abolished slavery in the French West Indies – although Napoleon reinstated it. In 1833, the British abolished slavery in the British West Indies. By the time of the Civil War, the United States was one of the four largest remaining slaveholding societies in the western world.

The late eighteenth and early nineteenth centuries had also witnessed the abolition of slavery in states north of Maryland. The gradual emancipation that followed the Revolution was gradual indeed; its course can be mapped in terms of dollars and cents. States where slavery provided only a small proportion of overall wealth passed laws freeing those born slaves not now but sometime in the future. So slavery continued to exist in many of these states right up till Thirteenth Amendment – although New Jersey, with an Orwellian strategy of doublespeak, renamed its slaves 'servants for life.' Emancipation stopped, however, south of Pennsylvania. While the issue might be raised – Virginia considered emancipation as late as the 1830s – states whose prosperity was based on slavery retained the institution albeit with sighs and handwringing that the proslavery generation to come would find embarrassing.

The generation that began the process of emancipation still worried about the proper disposition of African Americans. In 1816, Henry Clay and others founded the American Colonization Society, designed to 'return' to Africa black Americans, most of whom had been born in the United States. This meddling with Africa created Liberia, an African-American country modeled on Sierre Leone and sadly marred by assumptions of American superiority, but it had little impact on slavery in the United States. However, colonization remained a possible avenue to many white Americans; up until his death, Abraham Lincoln himself had leanings toward colonization.

By the 1820s, free African Americans in the North had formed at least fifty antislavery societies that demanded an immediate end to slavery and recognition of the rights of African Americans to remain in the United States. Not surprisingly, black abolitionists tended to be more militant than white ones and more willing to advocate the use of violence.

The Second Great Awakening, a widespread evangelical movement of the early nineteenth century, rejuvenated antislavery among white Americans. Convinced that slavery was a sin, not a social problem, abolitionists such as William Lloyd Garrison called not for gradual emancipation but for an immediate end to slavery. Abolitionists hoped to convert all Americans, including slaveholders, to a belief in slavery's sinfulness. The more radical among them also embraced the idea of equal rights for African Americans.

Abolitionists called the means by which they thought they must achieve their goals 'moral suasion.' One reason that they objected to slavery was that it was maintained by violence; that reasoning also made them reluctant to turn to the government to abolish slavery, as governments also rely on force. Thus, they initially relied more on reforming human souls than human laws. They engaged in a propaganda war against slavery, which was as notable for its invective against slaveholders and the South as it was for its charity toward the enslaved.

It is unlikely that slaveholders would have been receptive to abolitionist doctrine in any case. In the generation before the Civil War, the Old South developed a well-articulated, cogent proslavery ideology, one which was spread by writers and professors but most particularly by ministers, the intelligentsia of the South. Southerners argued that all great societies, whether ancient Egypt, classical Athens and Rome, biblical Israel, or England at the time of the Magna Carta, rested on coerced labor. Beyond claiming that the Bible justified slavery, they maintained that slavery was part of the divine plan for the redemption of Africa. As Mitchell Snay has shown, proslavery divines attempted to make slavery sacred. To war on slavery was, some southerners held, to war on God [30].

While the abolition movement continued through the Civil War, many antislavery advocates found it impossible to stick to its anti-political sentiments. By the 1830s, political abolition had made its appearance. The Liberty Party, formed in 1839, ran its first presidential candidate, James G.

Birney, in 1840. He received only 7,000 votes – one-third of one percent of the total number of votes cast.

Pure abolitionists had warned those considering politics that the political process would inevitably lead to a dilution of their stance on slavery. What emerged as the most effective antislavery strategy was the idea of Free Soil. Free Soil attacked slavery, particularly its expansion, as a threat to the independence and economic success of white Americans. The problem with slavery, according to this line of argument, was that it placed small farmers in competition for the land with wealthy slaveholders. Thus, if Americans wanted to reserve the West for honest labor hoping to rise, they must keep slavery out. In some cases, some advocates of Free Soil also remarked on what they perceived as another advantage of keeping slavery out of the Western territories – keeping African Americans out.

The concept of Free Soil was closely linked to Free Labor. Free Labor ideology may be viewed as capitalist ideology for workers and smallholders, but it was also a transformation of traditional republicanism. Where republicanism had placed economic independence as 'the greatest good', Free Labor ideology emphasized upward mobility. But the goal of this mobility – to become a farmer employing young men who would rise in their time – can hardly be equated with the aggressive industrial capitalism that, partially created by it, followed the Civil War.

The party that founded itself around Free Soil mainly served as a vehicle for the political aspirations of ex-President Martin van Buren. When he ran for president in 1846, van Buren received a healthy ten percent of the votes cast, hardly enough to make the Free Soil Party politically successful, but markedly more than the Liberty Party and its more aggressive antislavery policy had received.

The doctrine of Free Soil spread in response to the policies of the Polk administration. If judged by the fulfillment of his political goals, James K. Polk was perhaps the single most successful president in American history; he was certainly the last American president of vigor until Abraham Lincoln took office. A Democrat, Polk ran for the presidency promising to resolve boundary disputes between the United States and Great Britain in the northwest, and the United States and Mexico in the southwest; one slogan of his campaign, referring to the former dispute, was 'Fifty-Four Forty or Fight!'

Despite the bellicose slogan, Polk sensibly compromised with Britain, and the Canadian–American border in the west was established at the 49th parallel. Polk had no interest in entering a war the United States was unlikely to win. He had great interest, however, in entering a war he thought he could not lose, and so deliberately provoked a war with Mexico. 'Mr. Polk's War' led to the American capture of Mexico City, a resolution in favor of the United States of the Texas–Mexico border, and the acquisition of much of the southwest. Having so brilliantly served 'manifest destiny,' Polk refused to run for re-election and died shortly after leaving the presidency.

Like most other American wars, the Mexican War created great dissension within the United States. Besides the moral outrage created by America starting a war against a weaker neighbor, northerners raised questions about the war's purpose. Polk, they noted, had compromised the northern border, letting Canada take good land away from free American farmers. But where slavery desired to expand, Polk chose war. Henry David Thoreau wrote his 'Civil Disobedience,' an essay that later influenced Gandhi and Martin Luther King, in opposition to the Mexican War, and other northerners proclaimed the war as simply a war for slavery.

This widespread perception created particular problems for northern Democrats. After all, it was a Democratic president who stood accused of having put southern interests ahead of northern ones. In August 1846, a northern Democratic Congressman, David Wilmot, offered an amendment to an appropriations bill, saying that should any territory be acquired from the ongoing war with Mexico, it would remain closed to slavery.

Up until the Wilmot Proviso, both parties had worked hard and generally successfully to keep the issue of slavery out of national politics for a generation. The issue of the expansion of slavery had been considered closed by the Missouri Compromise of 1820. The so-called Gag Rule practically had kept antislavery petitions out of Congress from 1836 until 1844. But when David Wilmot introduced his amendment opposing slavery in any new territories, emotions that had been held just below the surface by Congressmen and other politicians exploded into protests, counter-protests, name-calling, and abuse. Northerners said that they had submitted too often to the South on the issue of slavery; southerners responded that perpetual northern insinuations about the immorality of slavery were offensive and that they had the same constitutional rights to bring their property into federal territories as did any other Americans.

Party allegiances were ignored when the House of Representatives voted on the Wilmot Proviso, and the northern majority passed the amendment. But in the end the Polk administration, calling on all the resources of Democratic Party discipline, defeated the measure. Nonetheless, the dominant issue of national politics for the next twenty years had been raised: the rights and wrongs of American slavery.

Although its importance as a topic in American political history has declined somewhat in the past three decades, the sectional conflict of the 1850s has been one of the most thoroughly studied periods in United States history. Once the notion of Free Soil emerged, increasing numbers of northerners felt they had a stake in restricting slavery and that the South made demands that insulted northern manliness. Southerners would continue to press their demands not simply as desires but as constitutional rights.

In 1850, when California sought admission to the Union as a free state, Henry Clay and Stephen Douglas, a border state Whig and a lower-North Democrat, were able to push a compromise through Congress that historian David M. Potter suggested might better be termed the *armistice* of 1850. Southerners demanded a national recognition of slavery that struck many northerners as tantamount to a nationalization of slavery. The Fugitive Slave Law of 1850, purportedly needed to stop the trickle of runaways, was championed not by the border slave states whose slaves fled north, but by a deep South intent on reminding the northern states and the federal government of their constitutional obligations toward slavery. The law exacerbated tensions between the North and South [22].

In 1854, when Congress had to organize the territory west and northwest of Missouri into Kansas and Nebraska, Stephen Douglas proposed eliminating the old Missouri Compromise line and allowing the people of the territories to determine if they would allow slavery. The repeal of the Missouri Compromise led to such protest in the North that a new political party, the Republican Party, arose in response; it would soon supplant the northern Whig Party and absorb their policy of economic development into its Free Soil doctrine. Later, the Republicans would also integrate much of the American Party, or Know-Nothings, with its nativist sentiment. Furthermore, the ambiguity of Douglas's 'popular sovereignty' created a contest in Kansas that turned into civil war by 1856, five years before the war between the Confederacy and the Union.

The failure of congressional policy to resolve the issue of slavery in the territories and the encouragement of Democratic President James Buchanan, a northern 'dough face' elected in a three-way race between the Democrats, the Know-Nothings, and the Republicans, persuaded the Supreme Court that it might put an end to the difficulties by judicial decree. In the Dred Scott decision, the Court ruled that the Missouri Compromise had always been unconstitutional and that there was no constitutional means by which slavery could be excluded from the territories. The Court also ruled that African Americans could not be American citizens.

Rather than settling the conflict, the Supreme Court decision escalated it. The most proslavery southerners, principally Democrats, felt their position newly legitimated by the Supreme Court. All those, in the South and the North, who sought compromise were alarmed to learn that popular sovereignty, admitted a practical failure in Kansas, was held unconstitutional as well. In particular, Stephen Douglas, who had planned to ride his masterful solution of the sectional conflict into the presidency, faced the discrediting of his doctrine and a revolt in the Democratic Party. He attempted to save popular sovereignty while accepting the Supreme Court decision, arguing that unless a territory passed a positive law recognizing slavery, the institution would be too unstable to survive there. Republicans, upon hearing that Free Soil policy was unconstitutional, rejected the Court's authority. Furthermore, as Dred Scott, the slave who sued for freedom, had been resident not only in a free territory but in a free state, Republicans such as Abraham Lincoln feared that the Supreme Court, by judicial fiat, would nationalize slavery, ruling that no state could make laws against it. When Georgia Senator Robert Toombs boasted he would some day call the roll of his slaves at the foot of Massachusetts's Bunker Hill monument, he referred to the right of transit he believed the Constitution gave to the slaveholder, but what northerners heard was a proclamation that slavery would be legal everywhere – and indeed, how long could slaves be held in a free state before they were no longer in transit?

Prior to the 1860 presidential election, in which the issue of slavery expansion would be crucial, two significant acts of violence occurred. First, on October 16, 1859, John Brown, an antislavery terrorist, tried to spark a slave insurrection by seizing a federal arsenal at Harper's Ferry, Virginia. Secondly, the Commonwealth of Virginia hanged John Brown not just for murder and inciting an insurrection, but on the impossible charge of treason against the state. Brown's attempt at insurrection, which black abolitionist Frederick Douglass had warned him against, would have been ludicrous except for the seventeen deaths it caused, but his ability to portray himself as a martyr made his trial and execution a superlative piece of antislavery propaganda. Mourned by many in the North, Brown appeared a harbinger of future abolitionist incendiarism to many white southerners who viewed Brown as a clear product of the Republican Party's inflammatory rhetoric, with its talk of a house divided and irrepressible conflict. Panic gripped the South. As poet Robert Penn Warren observed a hundred years later, a crazy man is only a widescale menace in a crazy society [35].

Brown's raid and execution helped create the emotional climate in which the presidential election of 1860 was held. The Republican Party nominated Abraham Lincoln, an improbable choice in many ways as Lincoln's political experience was limited to one term in Congress and what fame he had rested on an unsuccessful campaign against Stephen Douglas for the Senate. But he had shown himself to be an effective campaigner, he was an Illinoisan in an election in which that state was crucial, his Cooper Union speech demonstrated his ability to play well in the East, and he was too little known to have many enemies even in the South. While William H. Seward had been tainted by New York State's corruption and hurt by his association with 'irrepressible conflict,' Lincoln, whose 'house divided' speech was just as controversial, nonetheless had the important political virtue of 'electability.' His own party underestimated him.

The Democratic Party split into its two wings for the 1860 election. A majority of the party supported Stephen Douglas and his doctrine of popular sovereignty. Southern Democrats, however, demanded a federal slave code for the territories. They disrupted two successive conventions and ultimately nominated their own candidate, John Breckinridge of Kentucky, who ran on the Supreme Court's decision that slavery could not be prohibited in the territories. Meanwhile the regular party nominated Douglas.

A third 'party,' hardly worthy of the name, also nominated a presidential candidate. A remnant of the old Whig Party designated itself the Constitutional Union Party and ran John Bell of Tennessee. It offered no new ideas to resolve the sectional conflict, indeed could be said to have offered no ideas at all, but called for loyalty to the Constitution to preserve an imperilled Union.

For all practical purposes, the race was between Lincoln and Douglas in the North and Bell and Breckinridge in the South, although some southern Democrats remained loyal to the regular party. Bell, who represented the Union Party, ran better than Breckinridge in the upper South. Even though he received no votes in the southern states, where his name did not appear on the ballot, and only a plurality nationwide, Lincoln won the election.

In 1861, seven states of the lower South – South Carolina, Georgia, Florida, Alabama, Mississippi, Louisiana and Texas – attempted to secede from the United States because of Abraham Lincoln's election to the American presidency. All seven conventions that voted to take the South out of the Union proclaimed Lincoln's election a threat to slavery. Secessionists often disagreed as to how the Republican Party and the North at large would destroy slavery and how long the process would take, but they agreed that this election was the beginning of the end for slavery in the federal Union. Some secessionists argued that with a federal government unsympathic to slavery, the Fugitive Slave Law would never be enforced, thus lowering the value of slaves in the border states and ultimately throughout the South. Some, like Robert Toombs, argued that slavery must expand or perish, and saw in Lincoln's policy of disregarding the Dred Scott decision the end of slavery's expansion. Some feared that the Republicans would send new John Browns southward, and that the federal army would no longer fulfill its role in putting down insurrections. Others believed that through a careful use of patronage, Lincoln would succeed in building a Republican Party in the South itself, one which would claim the allegiance of white nonslaveholders, who might then abolish slavery by either federal or state action. All agreed that the election of Lincoln violated the spirit of the Constitution and justified regarding that compact as broken [*Doc. 1*].

Southern Unionists found themselves caught in a trap. As William J. Cooper, Jr., has shown, no southern politician could remain effective if it was thought he was weak in the defense of slavery. During the winter of 1860–61, very few southern Unionists unabashedly claimed the supremacy of the Union or denied the doctrine of secession. Instead, they argued that the South should wait for an overt act by the Lincoln administration or that every southern state should coordinate secession rather than any one state seceding on its own. Most southern Unionists, as it proved, were 'conditional Unionists,' not absolute Unionists. They succeeded in keeping the upper South in the Union for the time being, but the states of South Carolina, Georgia, Alabama, Florida, Mississippi, Louisiana, and Texas all announced their independence by spring 1861 [5].

The secession of individual states was followed by the attempt to create a new nation, the Confederate States of America. Representatives of the seven states met in Montgomery Alabama where they elected Mississippi planter, United States Senator, and former Secretary of War Jefferson Davis president. They also drafted both a provisional and then a permanent constitution for the Confederacy, one modeled on the United States Constitution. Finally, they created both the little-known Confederate regular army and the Confederate volunteer army. The seceded states and the new Confederacy also seized the property of the United States government, including forts. Most army commanders submitted without a struggle. In Charleston Harbor, however, southern-born Major Robert Anderson refused to surrender his garrison.

THE DECISION FOR WAR

Only in a rough way can it be said that secession led to war. Certainly, just as it is true 'no slavery, no secession,' it is also true 'no secession, no war.' But while the North's decision to go to war to preserve the Union now seems inevitable, it was no such thing. Until the inauguration of Lincoln, the South had reason to believe that the North would allow an independent Confederacy. Dividing up the territories would be difficult and the remaining United States probably would have refused the Confederacy all its territorial demands. Furthermore, a 'fugitive slave treaty' was an impossibility. Nonetheless, diplomats had settled disputes between Great Britain and its revolted colonies – why not between the United States and the Confederacy? Some abolitionists, including William Lloyd Garrison, the most famous of them all, welcomed secession. Other northerners agreed that the best policy was to 'let the erring sisters depart in peace.' President James Buchanan maintained that secession was unconstitutional, but that 'coercing a sovereign state' was equally unconstitutional. He proposed, as did others, concessions to the slaveholders' interests to persuade the South to rejoin the Union. What Henry Adams called 'the Great Secession Winter' led many secessionists to rejoice and unionists to despair at the administration's irresolution and the North's lethargy.

The inauguration of Lincoln and the subsequent firing on Fort Sumter changed the popular mood. Lincoln insisted that secession was illegal and that the federal government would maintain its rights and responsibilities in the so-called Confederacy. South Carolina claimed Sumter, a federal fort that sat on an island in Charleston Harbor. Lincoln would resupply the garrison of Fort Sumter to preserve it as a symbol of federal sovereignty.

Lincoln and other Unionists laid great emphasis on the Union, which was evoked not only as a political but also as an almost religious concept. Lincoln would later call the Union 'the last, best hope of mankind,' and he envisioned the nation extending backwards and forwards in time, from patriot ancestor to posterity, and spreading liberty throughout the world by example. Without Union, he believed, American freedom would be destroyed, by anarchy and its inevitable successor, tyranny. Democracy depended on the minority submitting to the majority, particularly when it was declared by an open, honest election. Furthermore, Lincoln and many other Unionists thought that secession was a bluff, and that once the South saw it could not prevail it would return to the Union. Or, Unionists argued, secession was a conspiracy foisted on the mass of southern citizens by a clique of ambitious politicians who would soon be repudiated by their followers.

An earlier generation of historians argued over whether Lincoln maneuvered the Confederacy into firing the first shot of the war at Fort Sumter. It is hard to see the relevance of the question; the Confederates backed themselves into a corner and Lincoln was happy enough to take advantage of the fact. South Carolina and the Confederacy raised the situation at Fort Sumter to the point of crisis. Since its Communist Revolution, Cuba has lived well enough with a major American military base at Guantanemo Bay; surely the Confederacy could have endured Fort Sumter. While the Confederate first shot may have given Lincoln the war spirit he required in the North, it also created the situation that brought the upper South into the Confederacy.

After the surrender of Fort Sumter, Lincoln called upon the state militia to muster 70,000 men into federal service for ninety days to suppress the Confederate insurrection. This call for troops prompted the secession of Virginia, North Carolina, Arkansas, Tennessee, and movements toward secession in Missouri and Maryland, which quick action by the US Army prevented [*Doc. 2*].

CHAPTER THREE

THE WAR, 1861–62

Once both the Confederacy and the Union had decided for war, each had to mobilize its resources and plan its strategy. While ignorant enthusiasts on both sides predicted a short war, both Lincoln and Davis and their advisers, civilian and military, knew better.

MOBILIZATION

Each side used more or less the same methods for mobilization. Instead of expanding their regular armies – and the Confederates had to create a regular army from scratch so they could refuse to expand it – both sides relied on a 'volunteer army,' a designation that remained in place even after the introduction of conscription. Both the 'nationalistic' North and the 'localistic' South, distinctions perhaps meaning more to historians than to people at the time, depended on the states to raise troops and the states on both sides relied in turn on its smaller political units, the towns and counties. Consequently, almost all Civil War regiments had a state designation – the 1st Virginia Cavalry, for example, or the 23rd Wisconsin Infantry. There were a few state brigades; General John Pope even advocated creating a separate Illinois army. Within the towns and counties, companies and regiments were formed by men of local prominence – politicians, planters, local businessmen, veterans of the Mexican War, ex-regular army officers. At the start of the war, enthusiasm for military service was so great there was no problem getting volunteers. Later, each side would be forced to turn to various inducements for volunteering and to the draft. (Both the Confederacy and the Union began conscripting men in 1862, but northern conscription, drafting men from state militia for nine months, was so weak that it is often mis-stated that the Union did not start drafting until 1863.) The states also often provided uniforms and weapons, the most important of which was the inexpensive single-shot smoothbore musket and the rifled musket. By the middle of the war, the rifled musket had become the standard long arm for both the Union and Confederate armies. The Union army could have adopted the breechloader, as the Prussians did in the Austrian War of 1866, or even the repeating rifle, for designs for these existed, but it was too conservative to do so. Use of repeaters at Chickamauga (1863) and Nashville (1864) reveal how much difference these weapons could make in battle.

The Union's material superiority over the Confederacy was marked and, there are those who have argued, determinative. The Union's population (over 22 million) outnumbered the Confederacy's (nine million) roughly five to two. Southern Unionists should be subtracted from the total number of Confederates, but then northerners who sympathized with the Confederacy should perhaps be added. More interesting is the question of enslaved southerners. On the one hand, they permitted the Confederacy to put a higher proportion of its white men into the army, and on the other hand, the Union enlisted almost 100,000 black southerners.

If the ratio of the Union's population to the Confederacy was impressive, other comparisons were far more so. The Union had a navy and the Confederacy had none; nor would they ever have in any real sense. The North produced far more food crops than the South. The North had roughly ten times the industry of the South, with 1.3 million industrial workers. In particular, American firearms and locomotives were almost entirely manufactured in the North. Yet the South was well along the road to industrialization, and managed to fulfill many of its war needs. The northern advantage from railroads and industry may have been less material than it was managerial – the Union had many more men whose business backgrounds gave them organizational experience. For example, one crucial element to Union success was its superior logistical capacity. This was not simply, as is often thought, a matter of its superior resources, although that certainly played a huge role. But Lincoln's second Secretary of War, E. M. Stanton, thought of himself as a businessman and committed the War Department to supplying the armies in a manner unprecedented in the history of war. Forever after, the US Army would be marked by its logistical abundance.

Both the Union and the Confederacy were remarkably slow to achieve a unified high command. In the Confederacy, Davis acted as general-in-chief for almost the entire war; and when Robert E. Lee received high command he did little with it. In the North, Lincoln understood the need for unity in command but it took him three years to find a commander both capable and willing to exercise it. At the war's start, Winfield Scott had been general-in-chief, but old age and the machinations of George B. McClellan had rendered his command meaningless. McClellan himself had held the top command until his insubordination lost it for him. Lincoln next appointed Henry Halleck general-in-chief, but Halleck chose to interpret his job as that of chief-of-staff; he advised Lincoln and usually advised him well, but he rarely commanded. Ulysses S. Grant's appointment to lieutenant general finally unified command for the Union.

One Confederate advantage was that the Union would be the invader, not because of the superiority of the tactical defensive – an invading army may maneuver in such a way that its opponent attacks, as was the case at the Seven Days' Battles, Shiloh, and the battles around Atlanta – but because of logistics. A long supply line was susceptible to disruption. Consequently, many Union soldiers would spend the bulk of their time guarding highways and railroads. Furthermore, the Confederacy was huge – 750,000 square miles of territory – with a long coastline that would prove difficult to blockade and a border with Mexico through which international trade would be conducted. Additionally, as the Lincoln administration proposed to reintegrate the southern states into the Union while waging war, large portions of the Union army would serve as forces of occupation. But this huge territory had no natural borders to protect it from invasion and deciding how best to defend it was as difficult as deciding the best means of invasion.

STRATEGY

The word 'strategy' has many meanings. It may refer to the plans for a military campaign, for the military conduct of a war, or for the overall political and military conduct of a war. In the Civil War, the political strategy controlled military strategy. The Union would win only if the Confederacy was destroyed as a political entity. As Unionists viewed the question as one of national integrity and viability, they could not accept a compromise peace. The Confederacy, conversely, only won if it established its independence; compromise was impossible for the Confederates as well. And after January 1, 1863, the preservation or destruction of slavery joined national sovereignty as the second principal issue to be decided by the war. A few Confederates and many Unionists might have been willing to compromise on the slavery issue, but neither the Lincoln nor the Davis administration would.

Initially, however, each side underestimated the commitment of the other. The Confederacy faced a difficult but nonetheless simple strategic problem. It did not have to invade the Union; it did not have to defeat the Union; it only had to outlast the Union. For the Confederates to win, all they had to do was not lose. What the best way of accomplishing this was, however, was unclear.

Union military strategy was initially predicated on a political assumption: the belief that secession was a ploy that lacked the support of the citizens of the new Confederacy. All that was necessary was to close the Confederacy's borders, stop up its ports, clear out the Mississippi River, and wait for the southern people, the white citizens, to repudiate their ambitious leaders. This strategy, developed by the aging general-in-chief of the army, Winfield Scott, was derisively known as the Anaconda Plan.

Elements of the Anaconda Plan would be followed to their conclusion –
the blockade, which required seizing Confederate ports to be effective, and
the conquest of the Mississippi. But the central assumption of the plan,
which was wrong in any case, never received its fair test. The Confederates
had positioned an army at Manassas, Virginia, only a few miles from
Washington, DC. Public expectation, which had to be gratified throughout
the war to maintain public support, was that this army should be defeated
immediately. Even Scott had recognized that northern war enthusiasm was
a principal obstacle to his plan. On July 21, 1861, a Union army attacked
this army. The Union and Confederate commanders had similar though not
identical plans for the battle – feint to the left, attack to the right – but the
Union attack got off first. The Union army lost and retreated to Washington
– fled might be a better word – and despite jubilation on the part of the
Confederacy and despair on the part of the Union, conditions in northern
Virginia returned to more or less what they had been before the battle. The
First Battle of Bull Run, the largest battle yet fought on American soil, led
to, as so many later battles would, a stalemate.

TACTICS

By 1861, the western world had reached the end of a long era in which
decisive battles might determine the outcome of a war. No Civil War battle
proved decisive the way Cannae was; no Civil War battle was decisive
except in the narrow technical sense of ending a campaign. The same flex-
ibility and firepower that allowed armies to execute flank assaults also
permitted armies to meet flank assaults successfully. Armies now were too
resilient to be destroyed in battle.

One misconception of many historians of the Civil War concerns the
impact of the rifled musket on Civil War combat. While the rifle certainly
increased the power of the tactical defense, the defense was already in
ascendancy. Archer Jones observes, 'As Europeans discovered into the
1850s, the muzzle-loading rifle seems to have made a difference of degree in
tactics rather than a difference in kind' [14 *p. 33*]. In any case, many Civil
War units started the war armed with smoothbore muskets. Furthermore,
Allan R. Millet and Peter Maslowki point out that 'the theoretical long-
range killing power of rifled weapons rarely came into play' in Civil War
battles. Few soldiers had been trained in long-range fire and the terrain on
which most battles were fought did not allow for it anyway [18 *p. 237*].

The military course of the Civil War was driven as much or more by
tactics than by operational strategy. A key problem facing both Union and
Confederate commanders was how to make a successful assault. Frontal
assaults were almost always failures, and when they succeeded, the cost in
blood to the attacker was enormous. Flank assaults did better, but were no

longer a sure means of success. In the First World War western front armies experimented with various ways to take the tactical offensive – creeping barrage, tanks, infiltration tactics. Except for one day at Spotsylvania, there was no equivalent experimentation during the Civil War.

But despite the superiority of the tactical defense, study of Civil War battles reveals that defenders often suffered much higher casualties than their advantage would suggest. Tactics had not reached the point where commanders recognized any solution to a break in the defensive lines other than a counter-attack. Thus a battle in which technically one side was on the defensive might see it suffer as many or more casualties as the attacker and still 'win' the battle. Conversely, a defending army which retreated might, while 'losing' the battle, inflict far more casualties than it incurred.

Finally, too stringent a 'military' analysis of what a given battle might accomplish may also mislead us. While we must avoid thinking that, say, Gettysburg could have led to a defeat of the Army of the Potomac, we must remember that battles won and lost had a profound influence on popular opinion. That said, we must also remember that had Pickett's Charge broken the Union line July 3, 1863 (something nearly impossible) and had a Union counter-attack failed to restore the line (something much more nearly impossible) and the Army of the Potomac had retreated, Lee would have faced an intact Union army the next day and had no chance of taking Baltimore, Philadelphia, or Washington, DC.

THE MILITARY COURSE OF THE WAR, 1861–62

After the First Battle of Bull Run, Lincoln replaced the commander of the newly defeated army outside Washington, the Army of the Potomac, with General George B. McClellan, who had achieved moderate success in western Virginia. Soon thereafter Winfield Scott resigned as general-in-chief. Despite Scott's opposition to McClellan – he preferred Henry W. Halleck – McClellan received that appointment as well, making him both the general-in-chief of all Union armies and the field commander of its largest single army. McClellan told the president, 'I can do it all.'

Scott's choice for general-in-chief, Henry W. Halleck, commanded in Missouri and southern Illinois. Ordered by McClellan to consolidate the Union position in Missouri, he did so, although that state would remain a site of bitter guerrilla war. During the early months of 1862, Halleck, known as 'Old Brains,' successfully planned operations against the much-admired and surprisingly incompetent Albert Sydney Johnston, and quickly captured Forts Henry and Donelson and maneuvered the Confederates out of Nashville. Halleck identified the Tennessee and Cumberland Rivers as the best routes to take for invading Kentucky and Tennessee, and, ultimately, to advance down the Mississippi River. His subordinate, U. S. Grant, commanded the army that implemented Halleck's strategy. It would have been well for the Union if, in the East, McClellan had assigned a field commander to do his fighting for him.

Historians, given to the narrative device of foreshadowing and knowing that Grant ultimately commanded the entire Union army, tend to write about the Forts Henry and Donelson Campaign as if he were the key figure, and Halleck little more than a nuisance. The campaigns, however, are far more accurately described as Halleck's, and he and Grant formed a nearly perfect team – planner and fighter. (In 1864, Sherman would execute Grant's plans and likewise be thought of as their originator.) Grant later stumbled at the Battle of Shiloh, where he allowed a Confederate force under Johnston and G. T. Beauregard to achieve total surprise; the fierce two-day battle, however, was a Union tactical victory, partly because of the timely arrival of General Don Carlos Buell's army. After Shiloh, Halleck took personal command of his army and slowly maneuvered the Confederates out of Corinth, Mississippi. The Lincoln administration was hardly deluded when it recognized ability and invited Halleck, not Grant, to Washington, DC for higher command in July 1862.

That higher command was available because long before July 1862, McClellan had lost the position of general-in-chief. McClellan disciplined and cared for the Army of the Potomac until it was a splendid force. Every bit the professional soldier, he did his best to resist civilian pressure to move before he believed his army was ready. Unfortunately, among the civilians he was prepared to ignore were Secretary of War Stanton and President Lincoln. While both Stanton and Lincoln had begun as warm supporters of 'the Young Napoleon,' as the autumn of 1861 and the winter of 1862 wore on, they worried they had a general who would drill, plan, and boast, but not fight. Furthermore, Lincoln had to deal with the radical wing of the Republican Party, including Stanton, who believed military expertise was less important than zeal for antislavery and zest for battle. In spring 1862, Lincoln not only removed McClellan from his position as general-in-chief, he reorganized his army into four corps – each commanded by a general acceptable to the Radicals. The Confederates opposing McClellan retreated toward Richmond. The Union's advance made McClellan look a little ridiculous when it turned out that many of their positions had been held by wooden guns.

Nonetheless, McClellan developed a plan of real brilliance to use against Richmond. In March and April he would move his army by sea to the so-called 'Peninsula' formed by the York and James Rivers, and advance east toward Richmond, with his army supplied by the navy and with his flanks protected by the two rivers. The threat to their capital would force the Confederates to attack – a fine plan to assume the strategic offensive and the tactical defensive.

Despite Stonewall Jackson's brilliant diversionary campaign in the Shenandoah Valley, which kept reinforcements from McClellan, the transfer of his army forced Confederate General Joseph Johnston to shift his army from northern Virginia to the Peninsula. Furthermore, on May 9, 1862, Johnston did launch an attack against the Army of the Potomac, resulting in heavier casualties for the Confederates than the Federals, a tactical stalemate, and temporarily disabling wounds for himself. With Johnston's injury, Jefferson Davis appointed his chief-of-staff R. E. Lee to assume command of the army defending Richmond. Like Johnston, Lee chose to attack. He planned a series of flank attacks that would turn the Union position, but poor battlefield coordination, even on the part of Jackson who had been summoned from the Valley, made the so-called Seven Days' Battle a series of frontal assaults. Nonetheless, Lee forced a panic-stricken McClellan to retreat down the Peninsula [*Doc. 3*].

In a very real sense, McClellan cannot be regarded as defeated in the Seven Days' Battles. His army was intact and his supply lines unbroken. Like the itsy-bitsy spider climbing up the water-spout, he could have again resumed his slow progress toward Richmond. But he appeared to have been defeated. Moreover, his demands for reinforcements before he would resume the campaign and his ludicrously inflated estimate of Confederate numbers persuaded Halleck, the new general-in-chief, that McClellan would remain inactive. Thus it made more sense to transfer troops from his command to the new Army of Virginia, composed of the forces so used to losing against Stonewall Jackson and commanded by General John Pope.

The delay that must accompany this movement, however, gave the initiative in the eastern theater to Lee. Lee seized this opportunity to lure Pope's army into battle before all the troops from the Peninsula arrived. Lee's Army of Northern Virginia perhaps reached its highest level of efficiency in the Second Bull Run Campaign. Jackson's corps, by raiding Pope's supplies, baited the trap, Lee's overall plan of campaign set the trap, and Longstreet's tactical ability swung the trap closed on August 30, 1862 at the site of the First Battle of Bull Run.

Having cleared Virginia of federal forces, Lee could have resumed the strategic defensive and waited to see if the Union army would invade again. But as always, Lee refused to give up the initiative. Throughout the war, his principal strategic concern was to 'derange' the Union army's 'plans and embarrass them.' By crossing the Potomac, he could position his army where it would threaten to turn the Union army's position should it advance toward Richmond, and if that army attacked the Army of Northern Virginia, the Confederates would have the benefit of the tactical defensive. Furthermore, he could resupply his army from the Maryland countryside. Finally, if he could keep his army in place long enough, its presence might have a significant effect on the northern elections that autumn. In the end, however, Lee moved north knowing that he was engaged on a raid on a gigantic scale, not a full-fledged invasion [*Doc. 4*].

At roughly the same time, the new Confederate commander in the west, Braxton Bragg, also decided to make a raid into Union-held Tennessee and Kentucky, in tandem with an advance by Kirby Smith's army in East Tennessee. The Union army, however, was well-supplied, and Buell was able to out-wait Bragg, although he could not prevent him from putting a Confederate governor into the governor's seat in Kentucky. Bragg had told a subordinate that 'this campaign must be won by marching, not fighting,' but on October 8, 1862, he stumbled into battle at Perryville, Kentucky. Following that inconclusive battle, Bragg moved his army south to re-establish his supply lines.

In Maryland, Lee had to bring his army home earlier than he had hoped. A copy of his orders came into the hands of McClellan, commander of the hastily reassembled Army of the Potomac. On September 17, in a series of poorly coordinated frontal assaults, McClellan attacked Lee's army in its position on Antietam Creek, outside Sharpsburg, Maryland. Tactically, the battle was poorly fought by both sides. Lee failed to augment the advantage of the defensive by building field fortifications; McClellan launched unco-ordinated attacks that allowed Lee to shift men from one part of the field to another and thus save his army. McClellan refused to renew the attack the next day and Lee eventually retreated across the Potomac River.

Both the Confederacy and the Union regarded the raids that Lee and Bragg made in 1862 as invasions, and thus when each Confederate army inevitably retreated after winning tactical victories at Antietam and Perryville, the Union celebrated victory while the Confederates mourned what they perceived as defeat. The Battle of Antietam has traditionally been regarded as one of the turning points of the war. In many ways it was. It certainly led to the withdrawal of Lee's army from Maryland, to McClellan's removal from command of the Army of the Potomac, and to Lincoln's issuing the Emancipation Proclamation. But Lee's army would have had to leave Maryland in any case; McClellan was removed because of his customary inaction after the victory, not because of the victory itself, and because of his opposition to emancipation, and he had been effectively removed from command before Lee's invasion; it is also hard to believe that Lincoln could have stalled on the Emancipation Proclamation much longer. The Union victory, such as it was, did not stop the British from considering intervention. Quite the contrary. As Howard Jones has shown, horror at the bloodshed and fear that Lincoln was provoking a slave insurrection on the Haitian model increased Britain's concern [15].

The Union made little military headway during the rest of 1862. Receiving command of the Army of the Potomac, General Ambrose Burnside fought the disastrous battle of Fredericksburg, which according to

Hattaway and Jones convinced Lincoln and Halleck that Richmond could not be taken. (Confederate General Joseph E. Johnston, unhappy not to have his army returned after his recuperation, said of Fredericksburg, 'What luck some people have. Nobody will come to attack me in such a place.') Grant's campaign against Vicksburg, Mississippi was disrupted by a cavalry raid on his supply depot. Only in Tennessee did the Union achieve success. General William Rosecrans, Buell's more aggressive replacement, repulsed a Confederate attack at Stone's River on December 31 – strategically another stalemate, but a symbolic victory for the New Year.

The war itself, however, was not stalemated, no matter how discouraged some northerners felt. In 1862, the Union had occupied vast tracts of territory claimed by the Confederacy, including enough of Tennessee and Louisiana to begin setting up loyal governments in those states, and New Orleans, the South's principal port. But the buoyancy of spring 1862 had been lost. The campaigns of first Jackson and then Lee in the East and Bragg's move into Kentucky made many northerners feel that the Confederacy had the initiative, an attitude that was reinforced by the failure of Union advances during autumn 1862.

Confederates recognized Union success perhaps more than northern citizens did. The most promising military strategy open to the Confederate army had proven to be that of raids, which disrupted Union offensives. Ironically, the further south the Union armies marched, the more vulnerable their supply lines became. But raids could never reclaim territory. In the eastern theater, Lee had demonstrated the difficulty the Army of the Potomac would have advancing through northern Virginia – another irony was that the commander of that Union army, whoever he might be, rarely had to worry about his logistics. The question many strategists, Beauregard chief among them, began to ask was whether or not the military stalemate in the eastern theater and the loss of Tennessee suggested that the Confederacy might better concentrate its forces in the West. But that would mean taking troops from the Army of Northern Virginia, something which Lee was unlikely to support. Lee argued that maintaining the stalemate in the East would turn the northern people against the war.

Whatever the stalemate in the East, the Union was winning the war in the West. And it would continue to do so, until its armies with western names – the Army of the Ohio, the Army of the Tennessee – arrived in North Carolina in the spring of 1865 and prepared to advance on Lee.

THE PROCESS TOWARD THE EMANCIPATION PROCLAMATION

In July 1861, shortly after the Union defeat at Bull Run, the House of Representatives passed a resolution introduced by Whig-turned-Democrat John J. Crittendan of the border state of Kentucky while the Senate passed another written by Tennessee Democrat Andrew Johnson, the only Senator remaining from all the seceding states. These resolutions proclaimed that the only reason the Union made war was to maintain the Constitution and the country's integrity. The resolutions also promised that there would be no war on slavery.

Yet in a year and a half, the war for the Union became a war against slavery as well. The Final Emancipation Proclamation issued by Lincoln on January 1, 1863 committed the Union to freeing all slaves in the remaining Confederate states. Even so, slaves in other areas, such as Louisiana, had to wait until these states drew up new constitutions to gain legal freedom, while slaves in states that never seceded remained slaves until the Thirteenth Amendment was ratified after the war was over.

However much some northerners, including perhaps even Lincoln himself, wanted to ignore slavery while restoring the Union, abolitionists, white and black, insisted on reminding them of its centrality to the crisis. More importantly, so did the enslaved themselves. Sure that a war against their masters must be a war for them, runaway slaves appeared seeking asylum at the lines of the Union armies [*Doc. 5*].

The Union army was fighting for the restoration of federal law throughout the country, but enforcing the Fugitive Slave Law seemed strange, particularly when masters who supported the rebellion demanded the return of their property. Lacking guidance from their superiors, commanders decided how to treat runaways on an *ad hoc* basis. Some sheltered runaways; some returned them. At Fortress Monroe in Virginia, General Benjamin Butler enunciated what became standard army policy. He refused to return slaves because he considered them 'contraband of war;' instead he put them to work on his fortifications. 'Contrabands' became the common term for those who escaped from slavery. Congress gave its blessing to Butler's policy when it passed the First Confiscation Act which called for the army to seize all slaves found working for the rebellion. Nonetheless, in loyal slave states such as Kentucky, the army continued to return runaway slaves to their owners, and in autumn 1861, many commanders unsuccessfully ordered slaves to stay out of their lines. The First Confiscation Act gave the army insufficient guidance for dealing with fugitives. In the Sea Islands, after all, it was masters who had run away, leaving behind slaves whom the Act did not touch: while their masters were disloyal, the enslaved people themselves had not been working directly for the military success of the rebellion.

With George McClellan as its commander, the Union army remained committed to leaving slavery alone. Nonetheless, Union soldiers and officers recognized that African Americans could aid the army. They volunteered information about the Confederates; they could labor with pick, shovel, and axe, digging trenches, building fortifications, clearing forest, chopping wood. Whatever their racial attitudes, soldiers learned that African Americans were useful. Furthermore, the work to which the army put slaves was the same as they had done for the Confederates.

In March 1862, Congress made it illegal for US soldiers to assist in returning fugitive slaves. But even this policy permitted commanders to allow slaveholders into their camps to pursue fugitives on their own. Not until Congress passed the Second Confiscation Act in July 1862 did the law make it illegal to return fugitive slaves who claimed their masters were disloyal. Far more important, however, the Second Confiscation Act emancipated all slaves with disloyal owners. The act also 'authorized' the president to enlist black soldiers, although in fact no such authorization was legally necessary.

With little enthusiasm from either his party or from slaveholders, Lincoln had been pursuing the chimera of compensated emancipation. After all, as he pointed out, the cost of making war far outstripped the cost of buying the entire slave population of the United States. Even as Congress abolished slavery in the District of Columbia, Lincoln tried to persuade the border states to take steps toward emancipation. Neither abolitionists nor slaveholders accepted his overtures. A few days after he signed the Second Confiscation Act into law, he revealed to his Cabinet that he had written the Emancipation Proclamation. In the proclamation, Lincoln invoked his powers as commander-in-chief and justified emancipation as a matter of military, not moral, necessity. Secretary of State Seward advised him to withhold the Proclamation until the Union could present it with news of a victory as well. Lincoln pocketed the Proclamation and for the next few weeks seemed to many antislavery northerners a monster of indifference to the slavery question. The Battle of Antietam provided Lincoln with something he at least could call a victory, and he issued the Preliminary Emancipation Proclamation. Even it gave the states in rebellion until the end of the year to return to the Union with slavery intact, but nobody, least of all Lincoln, thought that this offer would be accepted. Shallow detractors of the Proclamation sometimes argue that it freed no slave the day it was issued as Lincoln had no power in the Confederacy. No matter: it made the Union army ever after an army of liberation.

CHAPTER FOUR

THE UNION HOMEFRONT

Historians devoted to the notion that the Civil War was the watershed in American history would apply that to all aspects of American society. Thus they are reluctant to accept that which J. Matthew Gallman has demonstrated in his compelling work of historical synthesis *The North Fights the Civil War: The Home Front* (1994): the war accelerated existing social and economic trends in the North but hardly revolutionized its society. In the short term, the war did little for labor, women, or African Americans. Indeed, in the North it acted as a conservative force as much as anything, shifting more power and wealth to the emerging capitalist class.

THE VICTORY OF THE WHIGS

Barrington Moore labeled the Civil War a capitalist revolution. That is overstated. But it is true that this period committed America to financial capitalism, the growth of industry, and economic development. During the Civil War, the Republican Congress did more than simply orchestrate the greatest war the United States had yet fought. The Republicans also passed legislation that finally brought victory to their predecessors, the Whig Party. In the absence of a strong Democratic Party and with the new justification of the war powers, the economic vision of Alexander Hamilton and Henry Clay reigned [20].

When Lincoln took office, the Treasury was bankrupt. The United States depended on custom duties and, unable to collect them in the southern ports, was already running a deficit. With its Democratic economic policy, the United States lacked a national bank, a national currency, or a national system of taxation. With whatever Hamiltonian confidence in the support of the well-to-do they could muster, Republicans had to turn to the banking sector and the general public for loans. Bankers proved unsatisfactory, particularly the Wall Street community in heavily Democratic New York City, because they regarded the interest the government offered as too low. In Philadelphia, Ohio-born Jay Cooke, with his ties to Secretary of Treasury

Salmon P. Chase and Senator John Sherman, threw himself into selling bonds to the public, believing that the sheer volumes of sales would make up for the small profit he earned on each transaction. But the public loan, however an effective war-selling measure it might be, could not finance the war. The government was forced to issue paper-money – 'greenbacks.' Still the accomplishment of the Union in raising money was impressive: the war ended with no significant debt to Europe. Whatever cost American financial policies would inflict after 1865, the United States fought the Civil War with its own money.

The public's not entirely erroneous perception that the banking community wished to maintain its control over financial matters, even during a national crisis, helped overcome traditional hostility to paper-money and complaints that its issuance was unconstitutional. Chase and Congress envisioned the greenbacks as a temporary expedient, but also began moving toward a more nationally controlled currency system and the creation of banks with national characteristics. After the failure of the Second Bank of the United States in the 1830s, the federal government was finally trying again to centralize the nation's monetary system.

Wartime finances also required changes – some temporary, some permanent – in the United States' revenue system. Starting with the Morrell Tariff, which had been passed even as southern representatives left Congress, custom duties were raised on almost all imported goods, including raw materials. Republicans argued that the new tariffs benefited agriculture and mining interests as much as they did manufacturers. Congress also turned to internal taxes. Rejecting a direct tax on land as unfair to the western states, Congress imposed the first income tax as well as taxes on manufacturing. But after the war, taxes on manufacturing and incomes disappeared, while the tariff stayed high, providing protection for American industry. The Republicans succeeded in using the wartime emergency to erect the tariff barrier that industry had long demanded.

The Republican majority, however, did intend to help farmers. Indeed, the essence of Free Soil ideology was a belief in small prosperous farms in the territories. Congress passed the Homestead Act to encourage western settlement, created the Department of Agriculture, and granted the states land to fund agricultural colleges. But the Homestead Act eliminated land sales as a source of federal revenue (prior to the war they accounted for about nine percent of federal income) and helped ensure continued reliance on the tariff. Furthermore, only one acre in ten of federal land went to small farmers; as always in American history, speculators engrossed the rest.

Other actions favorable to economic development that were taken were laws encouraging immigration to the United States and the legislation and grants that permitted private enterprise to build the transcontinental railroad. Beyond these policies, and far more important, was the way that the national government became a giant consumer of all kinds of agricultural and industrial goods.

THE WAR ECONOMY

After a short depression caused by uncertainty about the future as much as anything else, the North's economy thrived during the war. The insatiable demands of the Union armed forces quickly made up for the temporary loss of the southern market. For example, the Union soldier required a new pair of shoes every two months, and a complete new uniform every four. Furthermore, even as workers enlisted in the army, farmers and manufacturers replaced them with machines and immigrants. Abraham Lincoln's December 1864 message to Congress boasted of the vitality of the Union, seemingly stronger after four years of war. He pointed out 'that we have more men now than we had when the war began; that we are not exhausted, nor in the process of exhaustion.' The Union could 'maintain the contest indefinitely.' One thing that the Confederacy could not beat was the fact that as the war went on, the North became stronger.

Despite the popular image of the North as an industrial society in conflict with an agricultural South, in 1860 almost three-fourths of its population lived in villages or on farms. There were well over one million farms in the North. Even the Northeast, home of American industry, had a far greater rural population than an urban one. While farm families suffered economically, as well as in so many other ways, from the loss of fathers and sons into the army, the overwhelming demand for food, wool and other agricultural products the war created made the 1860s a boomtime for northern agriculture. Furthermore, crop failures in Europe meant an expanded market for American foodstuffs there.

The agricultural sector met the new demand. Farmers mechanized to make up for the shortage of labor; for example, 165,000 McCormick reapers were sold during the war. Overall, the amount of farm machinery in use tripled. And while many farmers and their sons joined the Union army, thousands of European immigrants took their places. The North grew more wheat than the entire country had before the war. Northern corn also increased. Animal husbandry boomed. Cattle provided milk, meat, and hides for leather, hogs provided meat, sheep provided wool for blue uniforms, and even in this 'railroad war,' logistics relied ultimately on horses and mules.

With the exception of cotton textiles and to a lesser extent the shoe industry, the industries that processed agricultural goods also prospered. Factories turned hides into leather and leather into harnesses for mules and horses and brogans for soldiers. Besides wheat and corn, the Union army bought canned goods – milk, fruit, vegetables – on an enormous scale. The woollen industry doubled its output. With the Mississippi River closed until 1863, Cincinnati, Louisville and St Louis lost their share of the meat packing industry, and Chicago began its rise toward 'hog-butcher to the world.'

Of course industries whose production was overwhelmingly military in nature did well. For example, the du Pont powder works sold four million pounds of gunpowder to the military for almost one million dollars. Raw materials and finished goods alike required transportation, and railroads in particular flourished. At a charge of two cents per mile, Union soldiers also traveled by rail. The war saw little expansion in railroad mileage; most railroad companies had all they could do trying to keep the roads in repair.

As Eric Foner argues, far more important than the sheer number of goods produced during the war was the shift in financial power from the mercantile community to industrial entrepreneurs. Organization on this scale was new to the United States; the railroads had gone the furthest toward such organization but after the war industries such as steel would follow suit. The age of industrial capitalism, which would dominate American society until the twentieth century, was about to begin – encouraged, though not caused, by the Civil War. Richard Franklin Benzel argues that the creation of this new financial class resulted in what he calls 'self-limiting' nationalism that explains why postwar America possessed such a weak central state [3].

LABOR AND THE WAR ECONOMY

Free Labor ideology assumed a 'harmony of interests' between workers and employers. Republicans argued that there were no permanent classes in the United States – every laborer was an incipient entrepreneur and, if he worked hard, the ever-growing economy would surely reward him. The Democrats recognized the divide between labor and capital, but their proslavery attitudes undermined their strictures on class relations. The Union movement was still young and weak in 1860, and the war did little to strengthen it. Even as Free Labor ideology triumphed with the destruction of slavery, its limitations for an industrial nation were revealed.

With profits galore for legitimate businessmen and the army's demand for goods so fierce that commodities often escaped scrutiny, contractors could easily bilk the government with 'shoddy.' Originally 'shoddy' referred to a type of wool, composed of remnants and reclaimed wool, often simply pressed together. A uniform of shoddy, as some Union soldiers learned, could look presentable when issued, but might literally dissolve in a heavy rain. With the wartime market for inferior goods, 'shoddy' began to apply to anything poorly made, and the men who made fortunes selling such goods were called the 'shoddy aristocracy' – not just because their goods were inferior but because they seemed to real aristocrats what shoddy was to good wool. The *New York Herald* wrote: 'The world has seen its iron age, its silver age, its golden age, and its brazen age. This is the age of shoddy.' The most impressive swindle of the war was the gold hoax of 1864, in which a Brooklyn newspaper editor manipulated the Wall Street market by planting a phony message from Lincoln in two New York City newspapers.

Even if all contractors had been honest, soldiers and their families on fixed wages and workers whose wages lagged behind inflation would have resented those whom the war made rich anyway. After the war, men who served could see that emerging 'leaders of industry' were all too often those who stayed home and got their first breaks in the wartime economy. The future 'Star-Spangled Scotsman' Andrew Carnegie, who hired a substitute to avoid the draft, was only one among many who profited from a war in which they did not serve; his fellow shirkers and future millionaires included J. P. Morgan, John D. Rockefeller, Jay Gould, and George Pullman.

Furthermore, conspicuous consumption was the order of the day. One of the contradictions of the war economy was that even businessmen in the luxury trades prospered, as the shoddy aristocrats spent their wealth on the opera and theater, clothing, jewelry, and other new fashions, and the social season. What Mark Twain and Charles Dudley Warner labeled 'the gilded age' began during the war itself.

Farm workers did well during the war; their real income went up. The war's adverse effect on them would be felt as the war drove up the price of land and increased the farmer's dependency on machinery, making the entry costs for farm ownership much higher than before. Industrial workers, many of them women and children who were paid less than men to start, suffered a decline in real wages. So did soldiers, which mattered less to them while serving than it did to their families back home.

American factories had always employed women; Massachusetts's Lowell Girls were only the most famous. On the eve of the Civil War, women composed roughly one-fourth of industrial workers; during the war that proportion rose to one-third. Furthermore, the war stimulated the use of child labor. Manufacturers routinely hired children of seven and occasionally employed those even younger.

What few labor unions existed in 1860 supported the war for the Union. By 1864, the war's inequities encouraged workers to join new trade and craft unions, which led numerous, usually successful local strikes. But if strikes threatened war production, the federal government intervened. During the Civil War, the army began its work as the nation's strikebreaker, a role that would continue the remainder of the century. On at least two occasions, in Nashville and Louisville, the army forced strikers back to their jobs with the bayonet.

None of the problems faced by unorganized – or by slowly organizing – labor should suggest that the abolition of slavery, which the Union's war effort accomplished, was anything less than positive for northern labor or for the rights of labor around the world.

VOLUNTEERISM AND THE WORK OF WOMEN

Northern writers and intellectuals generally supported the war in an un-critical manner. Indeed, as improbable as it sounds, Ralph Waldo Emerson, sounding for all the world like Theodore Roosevelt, thought the war would discipline American youth and teach them self-sacrifice. As George Fredrickson has shown, the intellectual community called for greater obedi-ence to authority. The three great publishing writers of the period – Herman Melville, Nathaniel Hawthorne, and Walt Whitman – regarded the war with more suspicion, having never identified with Emersonian idealism in any case. One searches Emily Dickinson's letters in vain to learn what she made of the war, but the fourth great, although unpublished, writer of the Civil War era neglected the war, going so far as to write to Thomas Wentworth Higginson complaining about her publishing difficulties at the same time the Battles of Second Bull Run and Antietam were being fought. Whitman's *Drum-Taps* was the finest literary work to come out of the war, with his 'Over the Carnage Rose Prophetic a Voice' raising the most troubling questions about the meaning of a Union held together by force [*Doc. 6*]. Among those who reached adulthood during the 1860s, nobody matched Hawthorne, Whitman, Melville, and Dickinson as writers and the Civil War remained, in Daniel Aaron's telling phrase, 'the unwritten war' [1, 11].

The Union relied on the private sector to provide for its armies and navies, not just to furnish the material means of making war, but for much of the care of its soldiers. Volunteer associations performed some of the functions we would expect the government to do. These associations in turn were modeled on antebellum associations, and, like them, were generally officered by men but actually staffed far more by women. The most important of such associations was the United States Sanitary Commission, which far more than the army's Medical Bureau became the inspector of health, sanitation, and medical conditions of soldiers, as well as a leading supplier of medicines, clothing, and food. Even after April 1862, when Congress established a corp of medical inspectors, voluntary associations still acted as the watchdogs of soldiers' care. Benevolent associations sometimes surpassed a reluctant govern-ment in care for the freedpeople. The various commissions added contraband camps to the places they inspected. Northern African Americans also organ-ized to help the newly emancipated and black regiments. The YMCA formed an organization similar to the United States Christian Commission (USSC), which performed many of the same functions the USSC did, but also circulated Bibles and tracts in camps and hospitals. The Western Sanitary Commission, a part of the USSC, because of its size and independence, often seemed to be the tail that wagged the dog.

The most noticeable voluntary participants in the war effort – after the soldiers, most of whom were volunteers – were women nurses. Faced with unprecedented demands on its hospitals and doctors, the Union army turned to women to assume nursing duties. Clara Barton, the postwar founder of the American Red Cross, nursed soldiers of the Army of the Potomac with no formal military connection until late in the war; she also helped locate soldiers missing in action. Dorethea Dix, a prewar leader in institutional reform, offered to act as general supervisor of women nurses for the army. Her infamous demand that all women nurses be unattractive and over thirty years of age should not obscure the pioneering organiz-ational work she did in developing nursing as a field for women. It does, however, point to the way in which both women and men made women nurses acceptable by modeling the nurse–patient relationship on that of the mother to a son. Dix and other women nurses followed the advice of Florence Nightingale's recently published *Notes on Nursing* 'that every woman ... is a nurse' and that healing largely consisted of encouraging the patient while nature performed its work. Nightingale also believed that nursing could only be learned in a hospital. In any case, there was no particular training for nurses in antebellum America, and the women who volunteered, Union and Confederate, learned how to perform their duties by performing them.

The war summoned women from their homes into the factories and fields. Women also took over many teaching jobs formerly held by men, as well as government clerkships. Of course, prostitution flourished through-out the war; one Union soldier found a prostitute working in Fredericksburg, Virginia, whom he remembered from New York City. Thousands of women also worked as volunteers, sewing pillow cases and knitting socks, serving as nurses, raising money as members of benevolent societies, organizing petition campaigns, or traveling to Port Royal and other places in the occupied South to teach the freedpeople. The Woman's National Loyal League, organized by Susan B. Anthony and Elizabeth Cady Stanton, called for the abolition of slavery and for women's suffrage. Nonetheless, the war had little lasting impact upon the status of women in the North. As is usually the case, when the men returned home from the army, they took back their old jobs. Women's suffrage made little progress; much to Anthony and Stanton's anger, the Fifteen Amendment, which enfranchised black men, failed to extend the vote to women. Together, the Fourteenth and Fifteenth Amendments were the wedge that split the women's suffrage movement off from general reform movements, particularly those for the political rights of black men.

AFRICAN AMERICANS IN THE NORTH

While the war revolutionized the position of African Americans in the South, it had far less effect on those in the North. They remained subject to legal segregation and political disfranchisement – as well as occasional waves of mob violence. While it is true that service in the army became open to them – service in the navy had long been a possibility – Frederick Douglass's prediction that 'once let the black man get an eagle on his button, and a musket on his shoulder and bullets in his pocket, and there is no power on earth which can deny that he has earned the right to citizenship' [quoted in 17 *p. 349*] proved a chimera.

If the postwar South had sought a model for Jim Crow, it only needed to look to the prewar North. African Americans could vote only in five New England states – Connecticut was the exception – and, if they met the property qualification, in New York. Some states required African Americans to post bond for the privilege of residence; Iowa, Indiana, Illinois and Oregon supported 'Free Soil' by outlawing any African American presence entirely. In most of the North, African Americans were kept off juries and, in cases against white people, out of witness stands, out of public offices, and in segregation if they had access to hospitals, schools, and other public institutions at all. In most places, blacks riding public transportation, going to churches, or going to the theater had to sit in special 'colored' sections if they were let in at all. Interracial marriages were generally forbidden. Even cemeteries were segregated.

During the war, northern reformers pushed for change. Such success as they had was small but significant. Some cities integrated their streetcars. Some New England states desegregated their public schools. And some mid-Western states permitted African Americans the right of residence. But most reforms failed. Black suffrage made no gains during the war itself. Most states retained their Jim Crow laws and left African Americans as second-class citizens. Of course, the war had begun the shift in northern white attitudes that would allow for the passage of the Fourteenth and Fifteenth Amendments. In general, support for black civil and political rights was most often found on the federal level, as Congress worried more about the South with its large black minority than it did the role of the small numbers of African Americans in the North.

Furthermore, the war caused an increase in violence against African Americans. It was all too easy for some Americans to blame the war on black people. In several cities, most famously New York in the summer of 1863, white rioters murdered African Americans in the streets. (The New York riot began as a protest against conscription but rapidly turned racist; most of those killed, however, were rioters.)

POLITICS IN THE NORTH AND THE AUTUMN 1862 ELECTIONS

Politically, the war saw intense partisan struggle between Democrats and Republicans, but also profound divisions within the parties. There were War Democrats and Peace Democrats; Radical Republicans, conservatives, moderates. There was the question of slaveholding interests within the Union, particularly Kentucky, to consider. Most crucially, there was the issue of slavery to be resolved.

The start of the war witnessed a brief halt to party bickering. With only forty percent of the popular vote, President Lincoln had to tread warily. The Republicans, needing a consensus, offered leading roles in the war effort to Democrats and the Democrats, needing to avoid aspersions of disloyalty, accepted them. But the period of strict bipartisanship inevitably ended soon. For example, in July Congress passed the Crittenden–Johnson Resolutions, proclaiming that the only purpose of the war was the restoration of the Union and that the federal government had no intention of touching slavery. But a month later, when Congress passed the First Confiscation Act, a measure that could be construed as very mild antislavery, most Republicans supported the bill and most Democrats opposed it. With southern Democrats not in Congress but in the Confederacy, the Republicans had overwhelming strength in the Senate and the House of Representatives. In the early months of the war, however, a few southerners like John C. Breckinridge, soon to become a Confederate general, were still in Congress, where they could express fundamentally Confederate views on the issues of raising an army, fighting the war, and proper attitudes toward slavery.

Race relations proved one area of party rivalry, the Republicans coming to advocate immediate abolition south and north and the Democrats not only opposing emancipation but employing virulently racialist propaganda in electoral campaigns, even inventing the word 'miscegenation.' Another debate between the parties concerned civil liberties, with the Democrats arguing that by suppressing freedom of speech, the Lincoln administration was enslaving the white men of America at the same time it freed blacks. At the beginning of the war, Lincoln suspended the writ of habeas corpus in Maryland. Some in Congress resented this attack on civil liberties; others supported martial law but believed only Congress had the right to enact it. Finally, while the Democratic Party never championed secession, it did try to benefit from war-weariness, going so far as to characterize the war as a failure. In return, many Republicans regarded Democrats as traitors.

But party rivalries alone did not determine politics. As is often the case in American politics, or in any 'two-party' system, the centrists of both parties, in this case the War Democrats and the Lincolnian Republicans, had as much in common with one another as they did with the more extreme factions within their parties. The Republican Party never lacked for an anti-administration wing. A political cipher at his election, Lincoln was expected to be a weak president who would defer to his more experienced Cabinet, particularly William Seward and Salmon Chase. Lincoln soon showed Seward and Chase that he was president and leader of the party. But a vocal wing of the party, the group that came to be known as Radical Republicans, found Lincoln too cautious on racial issues such as emancipation and black military service. The Radicals would attempt to replace Lincoln as presidential nominee in 1864 with former General John C. Fremont.

At the same time, the Democratic Party developed two wings during the war, the so-called War Democrats and the Peace Democrats (the latter defamed as 'Copperheads' by Republicans, nomenclature amazingly still employed by historians). After all, the antebellum Republican Party had been a product of coalition politics. Some Democratic supporters of the war joined the Republican Party, something made easier by that party's masquerade as 'the Union' party as early as autumn 1861 and most notably in the 1864 presidential election. Others stayed in the party but cooperated with the president in Congress and with Republicans at the state level.

The first major set of elections during the war were Congressional and gubernatorial elections in the North during the autumn of 1862. The Republicans entered these political campaigns with fewer accomplishments than they wished. Northern confidence had risen too high during the spring victories; the setbacks of the summer, many Republicans feared and many Democrats hoped, would attract voters to the opposition party. Furthermore, the Democrats could campaign on anti-emancipation sentiment, as well as the administration's curtailment of civil liberties. Lincoln probably delayed relieving McClellan of command until November 7 so that the removal of that still popular general would not lose his party even more votes. The autumn elections, while hardly a disaster for the Republicans, did shift more power to the Democrats in Congress, as well as electing Horatio Seymour as governor of the crucial state of New York. The Democrats also gained control of the Illinois and Indiana state legislatures, although Governor Oliver Morton of the latter state, much like Charles I, dismissed the legislature and ruled without it. The Republicans lost elections in states which they had carried two years earlier. Nonetheless, the single most important outcome of the election was that the Republican Party still controlled Congress.

CHAPTER FIVE

THE SOUTH AND THE CONFEDERACY: INSTITUTIONS AND ALLEGIANCE

The true nature and purpose of the Confederacy remains the subject of heated debate among historians. This is no surprise, as the question must have puzzled Confederates themselves. Was the Confederacy the ends or the means? Was it a nation or was it only a device to protect slavery? Before the war, there had been southern nationalists; the war itself would create many more, the most important of whom was Jefferson Davis. But most southerners involved in politics would better be described as 'sectionalists' not nationalists. Sectionalists worried about the protection of southern interests, most particularly slavery, within the United States. They also worried about the South's status as a minority within the body politic, a status that seemed inevitable without the expansion of slavery. For sectionalists, secession was not a goal, it was a last resort. The Confederacy never had its nationalist moment.

Could a government with anti-central origins centralize enough to fight a modern war? Would a conservative revolution use revolutionary means? Frank Owsley claimed that too strict an adherance to the doctrine of states' rights defeated the Confederacy. Historian Emory Thomas argues that Confederates wanted victory so much that they revolutionized their society in an effort to achieve it. Kenneth Stampp believes that a moral uncertainty about slavery made many Confederates welcome defeat and emancipation [21, 33, 31].

One of the key divisions in Civil War studies is revealed by how a question is asked. Should we ask, 'How did the Confederacy lose?' or 'How did the Union win?' Those who raise the first question tend to look for internal explanations for Confederate defeat, while those who ask the second seek out external causes. And while it is not a necessary corollary, the former often concentrate on social history while the latter focus on military history, narrowly understood.

The Confederacy had to create both the economic, governmental and military institutions necessary for a political state and the loyalty necessary for a nation. It needed to achieve international recognition, repel the Union invasion, and generate loyalty among the people of the South. Yet the Confederacy failed at the first and ultimately at the second. And while Confederates sacrificed far more in their failed rebellion than Americans have at any other time, the Confederacy lost the allegiance of many southerners as the war continued and, in any cause, never claimed the allegiance of all.

INSTITUTIONS

The Diplomatic Front

While the Confederacy sought recognition even from the Vatican, the most important diplomatic question of the war was that of British intervention. Would Great Britain recognize the Confederacy and intervene on its behalf, perhaps by using its fleet to lift the Union blockade, perhaps by creating what a later generation would call 'a second front' by invading from Canada?

Confederates, initially optimistic about their chances for recognition, came to realize three paradoxes. First, Britain would not recognize the Confederacy and help establish its independence until it could be shown that the Confederacy could establish its independence without recognition. In August 1862, the foreign secretary, John Russell, wrote to James Mason, the Confederacy's man in London, that Britain would recognize the Confederacy after it had demonstrated 'an independence achieved by victory, and maintained by a successful resistance to all attempts to overthrow it' [*15 p. 145*]. Secondly, while Britain and other powers might be willing to mediate, if the Union accepted an offer of mediation, it would mean that the Union was so exhausted it could not continue the war in any case. Thirdly, while Napoleon III encouraged the Confederacy far more than the British did, he refused to act without British participation. Besides, almost everybody – British, Confederate, Union, other European powers, Mexico – distrusted Napoleon anyway. Confederate diplomats did approach Napoleon III, offering to recognize Archduke Maximillian as emperor of Mexico in exchange for French recognition of the Confederacy, but the Union dangled the same bait in exchange for France refusing to recognize the Confederacy.

To employ a southern locution, the Confederacy had 'a hand full of gimme and a mouth full of much-obliged.' They had little to offer European powers. The Confederacy withheld cotton from the world market, hoping to pressure Britain and France into intervention. By the time Confederates recognized the futility of that policy, much of their cotton was in Union possession and many southern ports, most notably New Orleans, in Union hands and open to trade with Europe.

Given that Great Britain failed even to recognize the Confederacy, the chances of British intervention seem slim indeed. While many northerners insisted that Britain wished for Confederate success, the central concern for the Palmerston government was with keeping Britain – and Britons – out of the war. Even the foolish provocation that the United States offered Great Britain in the so-called *Trent* affair led only to sabre-rattling, not war. Charles Francis Adams's success as minister to Britain owed more to the common goals the two countries shared, than to any diplomatic cunning on his part. But American inability or refusal to understand international law made Seward and Adams misinterpret many of Britain's actions, starting with Queen Victoria's proclamation of neutrality.

The only form of intervention seriously considered by Palmerston's government was mediation. Prime Minister Palmerston and Foreign Secretary Russell believed that the war, originally portrayed by Lincoln and Seward as unrelated to slavery, was a horrible and meaningless bloodbath. They wished to see it over. On humanitarian grounds, they wanted the war to end so the dying would cease; furthermore, they feared that the conflict would be transformed into slave insurrection and racial warfare. On economic grounds, they wanted the restoration of their trade with both North and South, and this concern grew as the cotton shortage began to affect Lancashire mills. The quickest route to peace, they thought, was Union recognition of the Confederacy.

Mediation would have been a failure. There simply was no possible compromise. The Confederacy would accept nothing less than independence. The Union would accept nothing less than reunion. While the British Cabinet had trouble understanding why the Union was so adamant, every time they discussed the terms they would propose to both North and South, they were unable to arrive at any satisfactory solution.

Conventional wisdom holds that the Confederate defeat at Antietam and the subsequent Emancipation Proclamation stopped British interest in recognizing the Confederacy. This misapprehension is understandable, as it was held by President Lincoln, Secretary of State Steward, and Ambassador Adams, none of whom were privy to what went on behind the scenes. Actually, Antietam and the Proclamation brought the British as close to intervention as they would ever come. The British characterized Antietam as horrific and indecisive, the Emancipation Proclamation as cynical, vindictive, and inflammatory. *The Times* wrote that Lincoln 'will appeal to the black blood of the African; he will whisper of the pleasures of spoil and of the gratification of yet fiercer instincts; and when blood begins to flow and shrieks come piercing through the darkness, Mr. Lincoln will wait till the rising flames tell that all is consummated, and then he will rub his hands and think that revenge is sweet' [15 *pp. 179–80*].

Nonetheless, when after Antietam, Napoleon III proposed that France, Britain, and Russia force the Union and the Confederacy to accept mediation, both the Russians and the British refused. In the wake of the Crimean

War, the British worried as much about France setting Russia against Britain as they did about the American war. Furthermore, if Britain went to war with the Union to impose mediation, it would create a bitter enemy and be left with unpalatable choices to make, such as the United States–Confederate States boundaries, the future of slavery, and so on. Nothing Great Britain could gain was remotely worth the risk of intervention. Ironically, it was the humanitarian Lord Russell, the Cabinet member most opposed to slavery, who most strongly advocated mediation, because of his horror at the war's cost and his fear of racial war that might follow immediate emancipation. He believed that an independent Confederacy, shorn of the 1850 Fugitive Slave Law, would finally institute its own gradual emancipation.

Some Confederates never relinquished the fantasy of British intervention. As late as March 1865, Mason asked Palmerston if the British would recognize the Confederacy if the slaves were emancipated. But long before that most Confederates understood that if they were to achieve independence, it would be by their efforts alone.

National Institutions

The Confederacy sent a few men overseas to represent its interest; its diplomatic institutions amounted to little more than these men and their suitcases. But Confederates quickly improvised domestic institutions, establishing a national government and a mass army. In many cases, such as the postal service, it would be fair to say the Confederates merely took over existing federal institutions and ran them, often with hardly a change. With their government modeled on that of the United States, they quickly set up the presidency and a Congress, although despite their constitution, they never did create a Supreme Court. The Confederates succeeded in creating the industries they needed to fight the war. They had less success in establishing the necessary fiscal institutions.

Confederate politics generally draw the scorn of historians, and most of it is deserved. President Davis, who had a difficult job, might be treated a little more gently; and most historians agree that, despite his shortcomings, the Confederacy had no other man who would have done as well. The Confederate Congress, however, never inspired much confidence, preferring to bicker, attack the president, and issue highsounding resolutions to tackling difficult questions such as taxation. Even with its 'business as usual' attitude, it did pass the laws necessary for mobilizing the Confederacy. Confederate governors often opposed the policies of the Richmond government, leading some historians to blame Confederate defeat on the states. But to do so overlooks the essential organizational tasks that the states did perform. Anyway, Lincoln faced recalcitrant governors and state legislatures too.

Initially, the Confederacy relied on a volunteer army. By 1862, however, Jefferson Davis and the Confederate Congress recognized that maintaining the army required conscription. In April, Congress passed a National Conscription Act, the first in American history. It called male white 'residents' – that is not just citizens – from ages eighteen to thirty-five into military service for three years. It also, however, allowed for the hiring of substitutes, just as the Union Conscription Act would, and exempted men in certain occupations judged necessary. For example, Congressmen, telegraph operators, railroad workers were exempt as well as college presidents and professors – the number of southern colleges boomed during the war. The most notorious exemption became known as the 'twenty-nigger' law: to keep plantations productive and slaves reliable, one white man was exempted for each plantation with twenty or more slaves.

Supplying the army was as difficult a problem as manning it; in 1863 Congress authorized what had been going on anyway, impressment. Designed to obtain necessary supplies, particularly foodstuffs for men, mules, and horses and so on, at reasonable prices, it forced farmers and planters to sell below the highly inflated market prices.

Compared to the North, the South started the war with little industry. War forced Confederate industrialization. Compared to the rest of the world, the 'backwards' American South was highly industrial; the Confederacy had a strong base which they developed into a functioning war machine. Ironically, it was food, not rifles and ammunition, that Confederate soldiers lacked as the war ran down.

The Richmond government did all it could to encourage industry. Private firms such as Virginia's Tredegar Iron Works and Georgia's Cook and Brother Armory prospered through the war. But unlike the Union War Department, which largely threw money at an existing industrial sector to meet its war needs, the Confederacy had to build and often operate the factories necessary for war production. The government also seized works formerly owned by the US government, such as the armory at Harper's Ferry, Virginia. The Departments of War and of the Navy managed most factories.

This wartime industrialization was a success. Emory Thomas judges that 'sometime during 1863, the Confederacy achieved, by its own estimate at least, self-sufficiency in military-industrial production' [34 *p. 206*]. Thomas points to Alabama's 1864 iron production – four times more iron than any other state, in the Union or out – the largest gunpowder works in America, and numerous other armories and foundries. He also admits that this rapid industrialization did not succeed everywhere. In particular, the Confederacy neither nationalized its railroads nor kept them in good repair. The Confederacy was better at producing goods than in getting them to where they were needed.

Confederate industrialization is too often seen as contradicting 'the Southern way of life.' Secessionists wanted an independent Confederacy, and southerners had long recognized the loss they sustained by having Britain and the North as their principal suppliers of manufactured goods. Economic independence should accompany political independence. Furthermore, much of antebellum state politics had focused on issues of economic development, principally constructing railroads – though from the point of view of the Confederacy, the states had not built enough.

In fiscal matters, the Confederacy neither innovated nor succeeded. The Confederacy employed two principal means to support itself: borrowing money and issuing it on paper – a billion and a half dollars. The Confederate government proved reluctant to tax its new citizens directly, but in effect it taxed them heavily through inflation. This inflation, and the resulting speculation, as well as the scarcity created by the Union blockade, contributed heavily to Confederate defeat, for it made it impossible for many white southerners to support themselves or to feed and clothe their slaves. As Stephen Ash has shown, civilians in the occupied South suffered from a peculiar monetary problem. Union authorities outlawed Confederate and state money but at the same time they flooded the local economy with greenbacks, forcing prices up. The only source of greenbacks for southerners was trading with or working for the Yankees. In most occupied towns and cities the Union combated privation by issuing rations to civilians or by other forms of relief [2].

Even though it ultimately failed, the army was the Confederacy's most successful institution. It provided popular heroes; its victories helped morale; and it kept the Confederacy alive for four years. When it surrendered, the Confederacy died.

ALLEGIANCE

White Unionists

Many white southerners, particularly in the mountains, were reluctant or unwilling to accept their new government. Among the white population, roughly ten percent still supported the Union after Fort Sumter. Perhaps if peace had followed secession, these Unionists would have slowly become loyal Confederates. The war and Confederate policies of conscription made that change in allegiance impossible.

Following a secession they held illegal, Virginia Unionists moved what they regarded as the true government of the state to Wheeling. The western counties of Virginia, with few slaveholders, had long resented the dominance of the east. The Wheeling government authorized the secession of the west from Virginia, ultimately creating the new state of West Virginia. Until the war ended, however, there remained in Virginia, albeit behind the lines of the Union army, a Unionist rump government. Meanwhile, roughly 25,000 West Virginians served in the Union army, while about 15,000 residents of the new state fought for the Confederacy.

Although it tried, East Tennessee never became its own state. It did produce some of the most noteworthy southern Unionists, including Parson Brownlow and Andrew Johnson. East Tennessee distressed Lincoln greatly, and he often urged the army to liberate its people from the Confederacy. Unfortunately, East Tennessee possessed little purely strategic value. A Unionist uprising early in the war received no support from the Union army. East Tennessee remained in nominal Confederate control for most of the war and, like Missouri, suffered heavily from guerilla warfare. Nonetheless, Tennessee provided more white soldiers to the Union army than any other Confederate state, an estimated 42,000.

Throughout Appalachia, the story was much the same. Southern Unionists rejected the Confederacy, fought guerilla operations, and enlisted in the Union army. For example, North Alabama raised a particularly effective Union cavalry regiment, the First Alabama Cavalry. Later in the war they were joined by former Confederates who resisted the draft or who wanted peace. Approximately 100,000 white southerners fought in the Union army; others fought the Confederacy as guerilas. Taking white Unionists and black southerners all together, a slight majority of the South's people opposed the Confederacy.

Slaveholders

As the secession movement was led by slaveholders and the Confederacy was designed to protect the peculiar institution, one might imagine that slaveholders remained united in support of the fledgling nation they created. As a class, they did, but as individuals they often looked to the main chance.

Secession itself had aroused dissent among some planters. Often the very wealthiest planters were Unionist. After all, they were doing quite well in the Union. Their economic interests were often diversified; they had investments north and south. Furthermore, their familial and social ties also crossed the boundaries between the North and South; the wealthiest southerners were also the most cosmopolitan. The more prescient also recognized that disunion would very likely bring an end to slavery.

The Confederacy was founded to protect slavery. During the war, some planters came to realize that protecting the institution of slavery was not the same as protecting their personal interest in slavery. Some Confederate policies put the 'property' of slaveholders at risk. The army impressed slaves to work on fortifications; this sometimes brought slaves close enough to Union lines to flee and even more often ruined their health. Planters began sending their slaves to remote places to avoid not just the Union army but Confederate impressment agents. Confederates with a gift for irony noted that some planters were willing to let their sons lose their lives, but not their slaves.

Confederate policy threatened loss to slave owners, but not nearly so much as the withdrawal of the protection of the army because of defeat or for other military purposes. Thus, as Lawrence N. Powell and Michael S. Wayne have shown, when the Confederacy could not defend the Mississippi River Valley, the planter class made accommodations with the Yankees; 'Many of them socialized with the enemy, reaped substantial benefits from the illicit cotton trade, and pledged their loyalty now to the one now the other, as personal advantage seemed to dictate' [23 p. 30]. As the Lincoln administration wooed white southerners, many planters 'rediscovered' their loyalty to the Union, some protesting they had always opposed secession and the Confederacy. And as the Lincoln administration reopened the cotton trade and cotton prices rose to more than a dollar a pound, many planters succumbed to the seductive qualities of US government-issued greenbacks. Signing an amnesty oath was a small price to pay for doing business.

Planters still within the Confederacy could also do business with the Yankees. New Orleans became the center of a large-scale cotton trade that crossed enemy lines. Once again, those officially concerned with the trade had to sign an oath of future loyalty to the Union, but planters unwilling to renounce the Confederacy could always trade through a more acquiescent friend or family member. Or they in turn could bribe Union officials; the huge profit on bales of cotton seduced northerners as well as southerners.

After Confederate defeat, planters remained at the top of southern society. In the absence of property confiscation, they held on to the best acreage in the South. As economist Gavin Wright observes, they changed from being 'labor-lords' to being 'land-lords.' While many planter families suffered terrible losses of fathers, sons, husbands, and brothers, it does seem as though, as a class, they got off lightly for leading the South into rebellion [37].

White farmers

Nonslaveholding farmers and their families made up the bulk of the white population of the South; the men from their farms composed the bulk of the Confederate army. And most slaveholders lived lives closer to those of the yeomen than those of the wealthy planter; the average slave-owning farm family owned only one slave. Paul Escott and others have argued that during the secession crisis, yeomen tended to be Unionist. The evidence for this is suggestive, not overwhelming. The argument relies on county-by-county voting patterns, which reflect antebellum political contention between the Up Country and the Black Belt over issues of economic development. They tell us nothing about the loyalties of yeomen living in the Black Belt [7].

Still, secession was born in part over worry about yeoman support of slavery. In the decade before the Civil War, the price of slaves had risen so much that entry into the slaveholding class was more difficult than before. This was one reason that a small number of radicals advocated reopening the African slave trade – something the Confederate constitution would bar. Some slaveholders feared that with a president in office, the Republicans could dispense patronage to nonslaveholders and extend its party to the South.

The yeomen made up not only the vast majority of the Confederate citizenry, they also composed the bulk of the Confederate army. Their loyalty was indispensable for the Confederate war effort. When their loyalty waned, as it did toward the end of the war, the Confederate armies evaporated. There is little reason to consider desertion from the army a complete repudiation of the Confederacy or its ideology. Men and women of the yeomanry often accused the Confederate government of favoritism toward the well-to-do, and they resented those planters and politicians who led them into rebellion but avoided their share of service and suffering. Their principal grievance, however, was that Confederate policy and Union invasion made it almost impossible to feed, clothe, and shelter their families and that as Sherman's March to the Sea demonstrated (see *p. 66–7*), the Confederate government could not protect soldiers' families in their absence. The war inflicted a disproportionate amount of misery on the small farmer and his family.

The 'twenty-nigger' law angered the yeomanry the most. Critics at the time and later historians often claimed that planters and their sons used the exemption to avoid military service. Nobody has yet done the research to demonstrate that planter sons were underrepresented in the army and I would be surprised if they were. For example, in Orange County, North Carolina most planters were too old to be in the army anyway, and their sons served in the same proportion as other men militarily eligible [16 *pp. 88–9*]. But the exemption favored the wealthy whether they chose to take advantage of it or not, and it gave the impression that the Confederacy favored the wealthy over its other citizens. One Confederate soldier wrote to his sister: 'I do not think it is right for me to go through the hardships of Camp life and the danger of Battle and others living at home enjoying life because they have a few negroes' [*Doc. 7*] [19].

Confederates had boasted that they could put a higher percentage of their white men into the army than could the Union because slaves could do the farming. This was grievously short-sighted. Many slaves fled to Union lines or slowed-down work. Furthermore, the Union decided to recruit black men. What concerns us here is a third reason: a large number of southern farms were worked not by black slaves but by white free labor. On yeoman farms, there were no slaves to raise crops when the men of the family were away. Women, older men, and children did their best to fill in, but they could not replace their menfolk entirely. Unlike in the North, agricultural machinery did not take up the slack; southern factories built guns and manufactured uniforms, not reapers.

Impressment increased the difficulties faced by many families. Davis himself acknowledged that impressment was 'so unequal in its operation, vexatious to the producer, injurious to the industrial interests, and productive of such discontent among the people as to only be justified by the existence of an absolute necessity' [7 p. 66]. The greatest inequality is obvious: the military only impressed food where the armies were. Some areas escaped impressment entirely, while others were sheared again and again. Besides impressing foodstuffs, the Confederate government also demanded a tax-in-kind, generally one-tenth of most crops.

The state governments, rather than the one at Richmond, attempted to support the families of soldiers, but the problem overwhelmed their efforts. They too faced the difficulties of taxation, inflation, and obtaining the basic necessities of life. Furthermore, the states created different systems of relief. For example, South Carolina relinquished soldiers' aid to individual counties, effectively putting support of soldiers' families on the yeomen themselves, while Alabama taxed the whole state for relief funds.

The news of their families' privations and the clear inability of either state or national government to relieve them forced soldiers to choose between their families and the Confederacy – or, more realistically, their families and the men with whom they served. In the winter of 1864–65, many soldiers decided their duties lay at home. Had the Confederacy continued to keep them well fed and clothed, perhaps more would have stayed at the front. Or, if a final victory against the Yankees had been merely conceivable in spring 1865, perhaps more would have remained in the ranks. But when wife and mothers called for husbands and sons to come home, many did. When the war ended, only 160,000 soldiers of the 359,000 enrolled in the books, were present for duty.

White Women

The principal debate in the history of antebellum southern women concerns the relative primacy of gender, class and race. Class more than gender points to the profound changes in the roles of southern white women during the war. Simply put, farm women were used to hard labor. Young single women of the planter class – the 'belles' – were not; and married planter women knew primarily the work of supervision and of health care. The shock of 'changing gender roles' was in some ways the shock of stepping out of the roles of one's class.

Historical judgements on Confederate women range from considering them as more devoted to the cause than their menfolk to arguing that their withdrawal of support from the cause doomed the Confederacy; indeed, depending on what time in the Confederacy's short existence is under discussion, some would argue both. Women cajoled men into volunteering; they implored them to return home. But here too class, age and marital status seem to take priority over gender: most of the cajolers on record were belles; most of the pleaders were farm wives.

Just as in the North, Confederate factories employed women. While southern culture may have been more resistant to white women working outside of the home than northern culture, Confederate manpower needs were greater than the Union's needs. In any case, the average women of the South, white or black, were used to hard work; and when the piedmont built its textile factories, white women were the first millhands. As in the North, too, southern women became nurses and hospital administrators. Sally Louisa Tompkins ran a private hospital in Richmond; in order to keep her in charge, Jefferson Davis appointed her a captain in the Confederate army.

Most white women, however, took over running farms or plantations. This was a profound departure for these women, particularly for those of the upper class. Asserting authority over enslaved men traditionally had been a masculine role, and it required a style of mastery uncongenial to women.

The demographics of the North and South did make a crucial difference in the experiences of American women. More southern women would remain heads of households because proportionately so many more southern men had died. More southern women would remain single as well. Furthermore, the destruction of slavery destroyed the role of 'plantation mistress'; nonetheless, the social mores of that role long outlived slavery.

George C. Rable, as well as Drew Gilpin Faust, has demonstrated that not only did the war make minimal change in the gender roles of southern ladies, but that these women themselves worked hard to maintain the continuity. 'By the end of the war,' he writes, 'many women wavered in their support of the Confederacy, but they seldom questioned the racial, class, and sexual dogma of their society' [25 p. x, 8]. Joan E. Cashin rightfully characterized antebellum southern women's culture as 'a culture of resignation.' The Civil War, if anything, enforced that sense of resignation [4 pp. 1–41].

Enslaved African Americans

From the firing on Fort Sumter on, the enslaved African Americans of the Confederacy were instinctive Unionists. Indeed, the first fugitives from slavery arrived at Fort Pickens, Florida before the firing on Fort Sumter. Throughout the war, they slowed their work, fled their masters and entered Union lines, and enlisted in the United States Colored Troops to fight for the freedom of all African Americans. If African Americans had accepted their enslavement, it is possible that the North would never have added emancipation to their goal of Union.

Despite proslavery ideologues who proclaimed the benefits of slavery to the enslaved, from the outbreak Confederates worried about the reaction of slaves to the war. For example, at the outbreak of the war, some Virginians wrote the Confederate War Department that 'the slave population is becoming restless and discontented' [2 *p. 14*]. Slave owners responded with harsher discipline. Furthermore, as Joseph P. Reidy has shown for Georgia, lawmakers tightened up the laws regulating slaves, a phenomenon true of the rest of the Confederacy as well. Reidy quotes a Macon slaveholder writing to prominent politician Howell Cobb: '[T]he fidelity of our colored population depends upon our success in effectually defending our soil ... Is anybody so blind as to feel sure that a vast majority of the slaves would not with avidity escape from bondage if they felt there was a power near to secure them that Boon' [26 *p. 113*]. John Brown's 1859 raid on Harper's Ferry created a widespread fear of insurrection and secession itself was accompanied by another such panic.

Confederate suspicions of slave attitudes increased as so many white men left the farms and plantations for military service. Few were confident that women and old men could control slaves, yet maintaining the viability of slavery now depended on them. Furthermore, with so many yeoman farmers in the army, most foodstuffs would have to be raised by slaves. And without the protection of white men, white women surrounded by slaves wondered if they were even safe [*Doc. 8*].

As racial subordination was the 'cornerstone' – to use Vice-President Alexander Stephens's phrase – of the Confederacy, African-American acquiescence was to be achieved through the traditional methods of coercion and custom. Yet the devotion of the Confederacy's resources, particularly its adult white men, to war meant the break-down of custom and diminished the threat of coercion. White southerners who remained on the plantations often complained that slaves grew unruly and impudent and that they did little work or refused to work at all. As the war continued, fewer masters could either bully or entice slaves into feigning loyalty. With the Confederate economy nearly in shambles, masters could no longer feed their slaves as well as before, nor could they protect them from Confederate impressment agents or keep the Yankees away.

United States Colored Troops

Despite the disproportionate fame of the 54th Massachusetts Regiment, the overwhelming majority of African-American soldiers came from the South, and most of them had been enslaved. Some came from the Confederacy; even more from the border states where enlistment was the only road to freedom during the war. Some volunteered; some were recruited at the barrel of a gun. The state and federal governments denied African Americans the right to enlist in white regiments. Instead, the army created 166 'colored' regiments, with black soldiers and white officers. The army also grossly underpaid black soldiers, disciplined them more severely, and fed and clothed them poorly compared to white soldiers.

Black regiments had been raised from the war's beginning, but the Lincoln administration always refused to accept them. When Generals David Hunter and John Phelps enlisted black soldiers, they were ordered to stop. One of the more cautious and conservative men to oversee a revolution, Lincoln both feared losing the support of proslavery Unionists, particularly in Kentucky, and preferred a gradual change in the status of African Americans. Black soldiers implied black citizens.

The Second Confiscation Act of 1862 authorized the president to employ African Americans in any capacity he saw fit, an authorization that, as it was not actually necessary, might better be regarded as a strong hint. Lincoln took the hint in his final Emancipation Proclamation. The Secretary of War, who prematurely had approved raising black regiments in South Carolina weeks earlier, began allowing the state governors of solidly Republican New England to enlist African Americans, but turned down a similar request from Ohio, where the Democrats might have gained political advantage. By the summer, however, black recruiting was widespread throughout the North.

The army itself recruited African Americans in the occupied South, although northern states, eager to have black southerners count toward their quota of troops, also sent agents among the freedpeople. The largest areas of the South accessible to recruiting agents – Tennessee, much of Louisiana, and the border states – were exempt from the provisions of the Emancipation Proclamation. Slaves in these areas, many of whom were ready to enlist, nonetheless fled to Union lines. In 1864, Congress passed an act making all black men subject to military service and conscription, thus allowing African Americans to gain their freedom by volunteering. In March 1865, Kentucky also passed a law declaring the immediate families of black soldiers free.

One use that Union commanders sympathetic to abolition made of black soldiers was liberating slaves, particularly in the coast areas of the South. Lincoln had predicted erroneously that just recruiting a black army would cause the Confederacy to collapse; presumably he had southern fears of another Haiti in mind. But this was hardly the rebellion that white southerners had feared for so long. Scenes from the Haitian Revolution were not replayed in Alabama or South Carolina. The Confederacy did regard the United States Colored Troops as slaves in rebellion. They denied black captives prisoner-of-war status, a decision which led to the shutdown of all prisoner exchange.

The official Confederate policy was that white officers commanding black soldiers were to be tried for insurrection by the Confederate government, while the soldiers themselves were to be turned over to state authorities for trial. In fact, no such trials took place. Far more important was the informal policy of not taking black prisoners at all. The massacre that took place at Fort Pillow and the refusal to take prisoners at the Battle of the Crater were only the two most famous incidents. In the Trans-Mississippi, Confederate general E. Kirby Smith was so angry at black soldiers and the complicated Confederate policy governing their treatment that he ordered that no quarter be offered to black soldiers.

Despite the racism in the Union army and the occasional savagery of the Confederate, the black military experience was largely positive. Former slaves and free men alike took pride in their service, and the news of emancipation was all the more joyful when delivered, as it often was in the latter years of the war, by African-American regiments. Active participation in the war proved crucial for black self-respect. The veterans knew that African Americans had not just been given their freedom; they had fought for it.

CHAPTER SIX

WAR AND POLITICS, 1863-64

MILITARY COURSE OF THE WAR, 1863-64

In September 1862, the Army of the Potomac, despite mishandling by General George B. McClellan, achieved at Antietam Creek, Maryland a victory sufficient for Abraham Lincoln to issue the Preliminary Emancipation Proclamation. If one searched for the 'key moment' of the Civil War, this would be it. Yet the Proclamation in itself was not enough to ensure Union victory. And Union victory was necessary for the survival of the country and for the destruction of slavery in the South. Political and social consequences rested on the military success of the war.

1863

As Hattaway and Jones have shown, after the battle of Fredericksburg, Lincoln and Halleck concluded that 'the Union could not hope to capture Richmond very quickly and probably could not capture it at all' [13 p. 348]. Not wishing to bog down the Army of the Potomac in a siege of Richmond, Lincoln and Halleck identified Lee's army as its true objective. In fact, while the Army of the Potomac would always attract the most attention, the Union war effort was shifting toward, to borrow Churchill's phrase, 'the soft under-belly' of the Confederacy – the Mississippi River in particular and the western theater in general. Spring 1863 saw Halleck transferring Burnside's 9th Corps from the Army of the Potomac to the West.

In the Mississippi Valley, Grant's army, with the cooperation of the navy, succeeded in investing Vicksburg, Mississippi by the end of May 1863. Both the navy and the army had taken bold chances: the first by sailing past the batteries of Vicksburg to ferry Grant's men from the west to the east side of the Mississippi; the second by campaigning with no logistical base.

Grant's campaign rivaled Jackson's in the Valley. He beat the Confederate forces opposing his landing, marched toward Jackson and beat an army sent to take his army from the rear, then, while it was retreating, turned back west toward the river, met the army guarding Vicksburg, drove it back into its fortifications and re-established contact with the Union fleet north of Vicksburg – all in two and a half weeks. Vicksburg was besieged and inevitably had to fall unless the Confederates sent a force that beat Grant's army. They never did.

Despite his new emphasis on the west, popular pressure again made Lincoln decide that the Army of the Potomac, now commanded by General 'Fightin' Joe' Hooker, must move against Lee. Hooker had restored much of the army's confidence; he gave furloughs, improved rations, and saw that the soldiers received their back pay. Furthermore, he had a sound plan of campaign drafted by General Montgomery Meigs for Burnside but still applicable. Finally, almost one-third of the Army of Northern Virginia was absent.

But as Hooker himself later explained, 'For once I lost confidence in Hooker' [13 *p. 382*]. After crossing the Rappahannock River and positioning the Army of the Potomac on Lee's flank, he allowed an unexpected flank attack by Stonewall Jackson's corps to convince him that his army was defeated. Even though Hooker had a strong defensive position and outnumbered the Army of Northern Virginia, he retreated, ending the Battle of Chancellorsville – a tactical victory for the Confederates and a boost to their morale, but one which cost them a far higher percentage of their army than it cost the Union, and one that restored the strategic *status quo*. They also lost Stonewall Jackson, accidentally shot by his own men.

In the summer of 1863, just as in the summer of 1862, Lee had regained the initiative in the eastern theater and once again used that initiative to move his newly-reorganized army northward. In 1863, his proposal met more internal opposition. With a stalemate in the East, did it make more sense to transfer part of Lee's army to either Tennessee or Mississippi? Wasn't Grant's siege at Vicksburg the greatest military threat? Lee, his prestige never higher, argued that an invasion of the North by his army would relieve the pressure on Vicksburg, and while that was unlikely, the president allowed him to proceed.

The invasion proved a disaster. Hampered by poor intelligence as it moved north into Maryland and Pennsylvania, Lee's army lost track of its enemy. When the Army of Northern Virginia blundered on to the Army of the Potomac at Gettysburg, Pennsylvania, a classic battle of encounter took place the first day, one that the Confederates won. Lee determined to continue fighting the next two days, attempting to dislodge the Union army, commanded by Hooker's replacement, General George Gordon Meade, from a strong position on Cemetery Ridge. Poor coordination doomed the ill-advised frontal assaults that culminated with the miscalled Pickett's charge on July 3, 1863. Paddy Griffith has written the best obituary for the Army of Northern Virginia's old tactics: 'At Gettysburg Lee discovered his formula for demoralizing the enemy by making attacks against the odds had finally outrun its usefulness. Unlike McClellan, Pope, and Hooker, Meade did not panic when his well equipped and well fortified army heard the Rebel yell rolling up and down the line' [12 *p. 38*]. Unable to attack any longer, Lee retreated from Gettysburg. Confederate withdrawal from Pennsylvania had been inevitable in any case. The surrender of Vicksburg (July 4) and Port Hudson (July 8) was a greater blow to the Confederacy than the defeat at Gettysburg.

After Gettysburg and Vicksburg, Halleck, with Lincoln's full approval, chose to keep the armies of Grant and Meade relatively idle, and to concentrate on other theaters of the war, particularly the trans-Mississippi, where Louisiana, Arkansas, and Texas seemed 'easy pickings' which could be reintegrated into the Union as loyal states. Grant would have preferred operations against Johnston, ultimately menacing Mobile, Alabama, or Atlanta, Georgia, but the good soldier obeyed his orders. In Tennessee, both Rosecrans and Burnside were to lead their armies further south; Rosecrans did so with overscrupulous concern for his logistics and nearly total confidence that Bragg's army would remain on the defensive. Meanwhile, Burnside moved slowly into the logistical nightmare of East Tennessee.

Now even Lee and Davis agreed with Beauregard and the so-called western concentration block. With Grant idle and Meade sending troops to the West, it was time to concentrate Confederate forces in Tennessee to defeat Rosecrans's army. Troops could be sent from the armies of both Lee and Johnston.

By the time Rosecrans had occupied Chattanooga, believing that he had maneuvered his way to a bloodless victory, Bragg was almost ready to attack his dispersed army. Fortunately, Rosecrans sensed something was up and that his army was vulnerable, and he started concentrating his troops. Still, while Bragg had to take the tactical offensive, he would do so with a numerical advantage, roughly 70,000 to 60,000, something the Confederates rarely enjoyed.

The Battle of Chickamauga started on September 19. That night, Longstreet arrived from Virginia with reinforcements for Bragg's army. The next day, the Confederates made frontal assaults and broke the Union lines. Rosecrans, in an unlucky hour that cost him his career and his reputation, lost his head and joined the general Union retreat toward Chattanooga. His subordinate commander, the Virginian George H. Thomas, established a defensive position that held back the Confederates. Once again, a defeated army proved resilient enough to save itself. The Confederates gained the ground but lost more men than the Union army. Despite their victory, the Confederates had achieved only a stalemate in Tennessee.

Nonetheless, Chickamauga left the Army of the Cumberland besieged in Chattanooga; Bragg cut off almost all of the city's supply routes. Lincoln responded sending 20,000 men from the Army of the Potomac to Rosecrans and by promoting Grant to command a new military department which left his old army under him but included the Army of the Cumberland. Sherman took immediate command of the Army of the Tennessee and Thomas replaced Rosecrans. In November, with Sherman's and Hooker's soldiers reinforcing the Army of the Cumberland, Grant was victorious at the Battles of Lookout Mountain and Missionary Ridge that sent Braxton Bragg and his army back into Georgia where his counter-offensive had begun.

After the Confederate defeat, Grant was promoted to general-in-chief of the Union armies and Bragg lost command of the Army of Tennessee, replaced, in the tired shuffle of Confederate generals, with Johnston, who had so mishandled the Confederate Department of the West. Meanwhile, at Chattanooga, Virginian George Thomas had taken it on himself to establish a military cemetery, much as was being done at Gettysburg, where Lincoln had spoken a few weeks earlier. When the chaplain in charge asked him if the dead should be buried in plots assigned to the states they represented – as at Gettysburg – Thomas thought and said, 'No, no, mix 'em up. I'm tired of states rights' [10 *vol. II, p. 866*].

1864–65

With the promotion of Grant to general-in-chief in March 1864, the Union finally achieved a unified command. But this was because Grant himself recognized the responsibilities of his position. Grant's promotion probably left Halleck with a sense of relief. Without hesitating, Grant took responsibility, even leaving his beloved western armies to come east so that he and nobody else would cope with the political pressure always brought to bear on the Army of the Potomac [*Doc. 9*].

Hattaway and Jones characterize Grant's favored strategy as one of exhaustion. 'Grant quite clearly understood the means for dealing with enemy armies, destroy their sources of supply and undermine their logistics until they withered away or became so feeble that they could be destroyed or brushed aside' [13 *p. 490*]. Even as lieutenant general, however, Grant found himself more constrained than he had expected. He would have preferred to command in the West, where he knew the men and the territory, but Congress had created his post so that he could face the great Lee. Grant also would have preferred raiding Lee's supply lines and forcing him out of Virginia, but the public wanted him to lead the Army of the Potomac directly against Lee's Army of Northern Virginia. Well aware that no battle against that army was likely to give the North what it wanted, Grant resurrected the idea of capturing Richmond as a symbolic victory. But he also haplessly created two images – 'the Butcher' for himself and, for Union strategy, a grim plan of attrition. The casualties of spring 1864 gutted the Army of the Potomac's morale.

Grant's hopes lay in the West. There Sherman commanded what would now be called an army group – James McPherson's Army of the Tennessee, George Thomas's Army of the Cumberland, and John Schofield's Army of the Ohio. Grant's orders made it clear that Sherman's mission was primarily a large-scale raid against the Confederacy's logistics. Grant told Sherman 'to get into the interior of the enemy's country as far as you can, inflicting all the damage you can against their war resources.' Along the way, however, Sherman was to 'break ... up' the Confederate army under Joseph Johnston. By winter 1864, Sherman succeeded, but only with the cooperation of Johnston's inept replacement General John Bell Hood [29 *Vol. II, p. 26*].

Meanwhile, General Nathaniel Banks's army was to capture Mobile and march toward Atlanta, which would already be threatened by Sherman's advance. Banks, however, had other plans for his army and pursued instead his ineffective Red River Campaign, which resulted not only in failure on its own terms but kept his army from its part in Grant's spring Campaign. The Red River Campaign was politically motivated and not just by Banks's presidential aspirations. Lincoln wanted Louisiana restored to the Union, Banks had already seen to the creation of its civil government, and clearing the state of rebels would destroy the rival Confederate government. Banks promised to do this and then attend to Mobile, but he moved too slowly. Halleck said this 'was about what should have been expected from a general so utterly destitute of military education and military capacity' [13 *p. 523*]. Cynics wrote off the Red River Campaign as one immense cotton speculation, corrupt from its genesis. By and large, the cynics were right.

Grant's plan for the Virginia Campaign was a miniature of his overall strategy. Grant ordered Meade to concentrate on Lee's army while General Benjamin Butler, commanding the Army of the James on the Peninsula, should threaten or even take Richmond. Other forces were to conduct raids against Lee's logistics in western Virginia and the Shenandoah Valley. While Grant would try, without much hope, to defeat Lee's army in battle, what he counted on was disrupting his supplies.

Technically, Meade commanded the Army of the Potomac and Grant commanded him. Grant also accompanied him. The course of the spring revealed some weakness in this arrangement. Grant did not always remember to issue commands through Meade, nor could he have. Furthermore, Meade had no authority over Burnside's Ninth Corps, even though it operated in conjunction with the Army of the Potomac.

On May 4, 1864, the Army of the Potomac crossed the Rapidan River. Neither Grant nor Meade expected Lee to oppose its advance toward Richmond; surely, with the Army of the James knocking at the door, Lee would retreat to protect the Confederate capital. The next day the Army of the Potomac attacked a fragment of Lee's army, confident that they could sweep it aside. But Lee counter-attacked and an all-out battle developed in the tangled forest that was called the Wilderness.

A year before, on this same ground, a Confederate counter-attack persuaded a shaken Joe Hooker to retreat back across the Rapidan. Grant was no Hooker. May 6 saw the Army of the Potomac and Burnside's Corps attacking, and a series of counter-attacks by the Army of Northern Virginia. Both Yankees and rebels dug in the next day. The battle had been a tactical defeat for the Union. From the point of view of the Union army, Grant's willingness to stay on this side of the river made the battle a victory; as for the Confederates, Grant's 17,500 casualties, 10,000 more than they suffered, and his failure to dislodge them from their position convinced them that they had defeated the Army of the Potomac. And in a sense, both sides were right. The Union forces had taken their first step toward forcing Lee to retreat toward Richmond to protect his supplies, while the Confederates had begun exacting the butcher's bill that might dishearten northern public opinion and cost the Republicans, even the president, the election only six months away.

Grant tried to turn Lee's right flank only to find, as he usually would, that the Confederates had moved faster. The ensuing battle at Spotsylvania Court House, one of the most horrifying in four years of horrifying combat, ended with another Union tactical defeat, another long list of Union casualties, and the Army of the Potomac still seeking a road to Richmond. Lee's army would be there to oppose them every step of the way, because Butler had bungled his operation on the James River.

Perhaps because of the unexpected success of the Army of the Cumberland's frontal assault at Missionary Ridge, Grant had resorted to such an attack at Spotsylvania. On June 3, 1864, he tried again at Cold Harbor – his biggest blunder the entire war. The soldiers of the Army of the Potomac knew better than their commander; before they made the assault against the Army of Northern Virginia's trenches, many of them improvised dog tags so their bodies could be identified. One soldier made a final diary entry: 'June 3. Cold Harbor. I was killed.' The Union lost 7,000 men in fifteen minutes; by the end of the morning some soldiers and officers, including General W. F. Smith, commanding the 18th Corps, were refusing commands to renew the attack [17 *p. 422*].

The Battle of Cold Harbor helped demoralize many soldiers of the Army of the Potomac, although by this point in the war, many veterans would have become 'old lags' anyway. Certainly June 3, 1864, saw the last general charge made by that army. Grant returned to maneuvering against Lee's supply lines, seeking to approach Richmond from the south where Butler had failed so thoroughly. But the 18th Corps, which led the movement against Petersburg, was understandably cautious. The Confederates saved Petersburg and their supply lines, and the Union armies settled into a siege of Richmond. At the end of July Burnside's Corp literally blew a hole in the Confederate lines by exploding a mine under them, but this attempt to capture their trenches failed, and the Battle of Crater became best known for the glee with which Confederate soldiers shot down black troops 'like fish in a barrel,' caught in a trap of the Union's devising. It also revealed again the futility of frontal assaults.

From the time of crossing the river to the day the Petersburg offensive petered out, Grant's armies had lost over 60,000 soldiers – twice as many as had the Confederates and roughly the same number of soldiers who had composed Lee's army at the start of the campaign. Grant himself had gained his reputation of 'the Butcher.' Furthermore, the frontal assaults had de-moralized the soldiers. 'One of Grant's staff officers noted: "Troops do not fight as well as when we started. Best officers and best men gone – losses enormous"' [13 *p. 592*].

In the West, Sherman's army group had accomplished at least as much with far fewer losses. With twice as many men as Johnston, they outflanked his army, forcing it out of position time and time again, chasing it from Resaca to Kennesaw Mountain. Sherman refused to attack Johnston's army when it was entrenched and Johnston could not be lured into attacking Sherman's army. Skirmishing was constant; battle rare. Of course, this judgement goes by 1864 standards. At the First Battle of Bull Run, Union casualties were a little under 3,000, and Confederate a little under 2,000. At Resaca, Union casualties were about 6,000, Confederate 5,000. Gettysburg, Shiloh, Chickamauga had changed the measure.

On June 27, at Kennesaw Mountain, Sherman launched a frontal assault against Johnston's entrenchments. It failed. Sherman claimed that both the Confederates and the Federals needed to be reminded that the Union army would attack. Perhaps. The attack at Kennesaw Mountain, however, was poorly coordinated and Sherman returned to maneuvering Johnston's army out of position. By July 8, Union soldiers could see Atlanta.

After the war, Sherman said he admired Joseph Johnston as a comman-der. But Johnston's reputation rests on his masterful handling of a slow retreat. President Davis wanted Johnston to stop Sherman's advance, not merely slow it down. Johnston's subordinate, John Bell Hood, schemed to replace him. On July 17, Davis gave Hood command of the Army of Tennessee. Three days later, Hood began the series of assaults which, as much as anything Sherman did, forced the Army of Tennessee out of Atlanta. Nonetheless, Hood held on to the city until September.

Another campaign, as dramatic as the north Georgia one, had begun in the East even as Grant's dead and wounded lay before the Confederate lines at Cold Harbor. Lee risked a corps of the Army of Northern Virginia to clear the Shenandoah Valley of Union soldiers and save its wheat crop. Commanded by Jubal Early, it chased the Yankees from the Valley and began a raid toward Washington, DC. It reached the outskirts of Washington on July 11, but retreated the next day. The defenses of the city had been reenforced by two divisions of the Army of the Potomac's 6th Corps.

Grant had brought Philip Sheridan east from the Army of the Cumberland and told him to reorganize the Army of the Potomac's cavalry, which he did with marked success. In August 1864, Grant gave Sheridan command of the Army of the Shenandoah, with orders to force the Confederates out of the Valley while destroying all crops and other provisions. Sheridan's army defeated Early's in September and devastated the Valley. A surprise Confederate attack at Cedar Creek on October 19, 1864 failed to dislodge Sheridan's army. For the few months remaining in the war, Sheridan's cavalry would raid Lee's supply lines. Eventually, at the Battle of Five Forks (April 1, 1865), Sheridan's troops would break Pickett's Confederates and flank Lee out of his position at Petersburg, forcing the retreat toward Appomattox.

CONFEDERATE POLITICS, 1864

The authors of the Confederate constitution regarded the politicking that the American president did seeking a second term as a danger to good government. Consequently, the Confederate president served only one six-year term. Unlike Abraham Lincoln, Jefferson Davis faced no re-election campaign during 1864. However, he did face the Second Confederate Congress, elected in the 1863 autumn elections. Davis had always had his difficulties with Congress, but the anti-administration feeling was stronger than before. Furthermore, North Carolina had sent men to Richmond who introduced peace resolutions during the first session of the new Congress.

Discussion of peace, to be obtained if necessary through separate state negotiations, became the focus of Confederate politics in 1864. The summer before, in North Carolina, newspaper editor William W. Holden had started a peace movement that Governor Zebulon Vance thought would try to return the state to the Union by holding a general convention for that purpose in May 1864. North Carolinians had elected several peace candidates to their state legislature as well. Vance ran successfully against Holden for re-election in the spring of 1863, but only by portraying himself as simultaneously a loyal Confederate and a peace advocate. In February 1864, Davis demanded suspension of the writ of habeas corpus because of the existence of secret peace societies in the Confederacy; in March, Governor Joseph Brown of Georgia, a breathtaking political chameleon, called a special legislative session in order to denounce Congress's suspension of the writ, and to demand peace negotiations. In May, some Congressmen proposed that the Confederacy should return to the Union if it promised the perpetuation of slavery.

It was resistance to the Richmond government by the states that caused the greatest problem for Davis. Historian Frank Owsley famously observed that the Confederacy's tombstone should read 'died of states' rights.' Few historians would go so far now, but it is true that during the latter part of the war, state governors grew particularly uncooperative, opposing conscription, refusing supplies needed by the army (using them instead for poor relief) and defending their actions with states' rights theory [21 *p. 1*].

Not many white men of military age were left to conscript anyway. So in January 1864, the Irish-born Confederate general Patrick Cleburne prepared a memorial proposing that the Confederacy emancipate its slaves and recruit black men as soldiers. Cleburne's commander declined to send the memorial any further up the chain of command, but Davis learned of it anyway. Davis's response was to order the 'suppression, not only of the memorial itself, but likewise of all discussion and controversy respecting or growing out of it' [34 *p. 263*]. Yet by November, Davis himself recommended a similar plan to Congress, buying slaves to serve in the military, possibly as soldiers, with manumission as their reward. He sought authorization to start with 40,000 African American men. Congress refused.

THE RE-ELECTION OF LINCOLN: A TURNING POINT?

In August 1864, with Sherman's army seemingly stalled before Atlanta and with Grant's army dug in around Petersburg, Lincoln concluded that his odds of winning re-election were inconsiderable. Apparently, the recent naval victory at Mobile Bay failed to encourage him. Lincoln proceeded oddly, summoning his Cabinet and insisting that they sign a statement which he refused to let them read. The statement called for cooperation with the new president 'to save the Union between the election and the inauguration; as he will have secured his election on such ground that he can not possibly save it afterwards' [17 *p. 440*]. Perhaps this queer episode was a product of Lincoln's notorious melancholia. Earlier that year, however, Lincoln had seen that some members of his party, including an office-holder in his Cabinet, felt no personal loyalty to him.

Among the Radical Republicans, first Secretary of the Treasury Salmon P. Chase, then John C. Fremont challenged Lincoln. Lincoln and the Republican National Committee squelched Chase's candidacy; Chase remained in the Cabinet and in the party. Lincoln soon rewarded – or punished – Chase with an appointment to the Supreme Court. The Republican Party nominated Lincoln as its presidential candidate in June 1864. Fremont, however, was willing to run as the candidate of a new party, the Radical Democracy.

Many reformers, including Elizabeth Cady Stanton, Susan B. Anthony, Wendell Phillips, and Frederick Douglass supported Fremont and a platform that advocated national emancipation, equal civil rights for African Americans, and confiscation of land. Some cynical Democrats supported Fremont as a spoiler.

Sherman's army took Atlanta in early September. Less than two weeks later, Fremont withdrew from the race. The Radical vote would go to Lincoln. It had nowhere else to go. Lincoln also recruited a southern Democrat, Andrew Johnson, as his vice-presidential nominee. This move to attract Democratic voters was one of the most unfortunate political tactics in American history, for it made Johnson president during the beginning of Reconstruction.

The Democratic Party, which had been formed around the military hero Andrew Jackson, nominated the less heroic George B. McClellan. McClellan's public protests against emancipation had continued after his dismissal from the army. He would have sacrificed emancipation for reunion. He would not have sacrificed the Union for peace. But the Democrats saddled McClellan with vice-presidential candidate George Pendleton, a Peace Democrat, and with a platform advocating an armistice and a peace convention [*Doc. 10*].

The election of 1864 was an ugly one. Republicans branded Democrats from McClellan down as traitors. Democrats, coining the word 'miscegenation', portrayed Republicans as advocates of racial mixing. In the end, though, the election was not even close. Lincoln took fifty-five percent of the popular vote, including eighty percent of the soldier vote. One wonders at what to marvel more: a national government allowing elections in the middle of a rebellion on a gigantic scale; a government allowing its soldiers to vote in an election many administration officials feared might bring peace without victory; or the veterans themselves voting in overwhelming numbers for the continuation of the war.

Historian James McPherson has called the re-election of Lincoln 'the third turning point' of the Civil War [17]. (It would be a place where things might have turned and did not, as the progress and conduct of the war went on much as it had before.) McPherson has argued that without the fall of Atlanta, the North might have given up on the war. Other historians attribute Lincoln's re-election to Union military victories. This is possible but not certain. American political culture exalted party loyalty far more in the nineteenth century than in the twentieth century, and most Americans voted the same way in 1864 as they had in previous elections. Lincoln's election victory hardly suggests he barely sneaked by or had ever had much of a chance of losing.

Nor would the nomination of either Chase or Fremont have meant certain defeat for the Republicans. If elected president, either of these candidates would have continued the war against the Confederacy. American historians have trouble remembering that to Chase and others, Lincoln was a man, not a national icon. They also have trouble imagining any other president winning the war. If Fremont and Lincoln had both remained in the race, however, it is possible that the Republican vote would have been split and a Democrat elected.

The commonly accepted belief that the election of McClellan would have meant Confederate independence ignores certain factors. First, as Lincoln himself acknowledged, he would have had until March to win the war, and by March the war was clearly won. The re-election of Lincoln did weaken the already feeble Confederate will to continue fighting, but McClellan's insistence on peace-with-reunion had already discouraged many. Secondly, despite the Democratic Party's peace platform, McClellan himself insisted on a restored Union. Thirdly, as of January 1, 1865, there was hardly a Confederate army left to fight.

CHAPTER SEVEN

A MORE PERFECT UNION?

THE LAST CAMPAIGNS

> It is over but they will not let it be over.
> (Stephen Vincent Benet, *John Brown's Body*)

Applying the phrase 'war effort' to the Confederacy after the re-election of Lincoln would be flattery. There were few efforts made to stop the inexorable Union advance, and calls for renewed defiance rang out as if their speakers played in opera *buffe*. But if it was a comedy, it was black comedy, and the greatest comedian was General John Bell Hood who succeeded in wrecking the Army of Tennessee by orders not only foolhardy but malicious.

After the fall of Atlanta, Hood had tried to lure Sherman's army group away from Atlanta, maneuvering his army so that he usually avoided battle. Sherman finally grew weary of his fruitless chase after Hood. He detached two corps under the command of General Thomas, who was instructed to defend Tennessee. On November 15, 1864, Sherman's army set out on its march from Atlanta to the sea. Instead of opposing the march, Hood invaded Tennessee.

When Hood marched his army away from Sherman's, he expected that he would be followed. When Sherman continued southeast, Hood, with no clear idea what to do, parked his army in northern Alabama. After a delay of several weeks, he began the advance into Tennessee that Sherman had already foreseen. Hood undertook the last Confederate raid, which he believed would punch through Union-occupied Tennessee and Kentucky all the way to the Ohio River, where he would threaten the Mid-West and would be in a position to march to the relief of Lee's army. Hood proclaimed the invincibility of the tactical offensive in a war that had demonstrated the reverse and he attributed defeat to what he viewed as a lack of elan among his soldiers. Furthermore, he ignored the Union's numerical superiority in Kentucky.

Sometimes it seemed that Hood hated his soldiers for letting him down. At Franklin, Tennessee, on November 30, 1864, he ordered the last grand frontal assault of the war. It failed. Yet when the Union forces at Franklin moved toward Nashville to rejoin the bulk of the Union army, Hood decided to pursue. When he reached Nashville, even Hood knew it would be crazy to attack. So he tarried just south of the city, while the methodical George Thomas prepared the Army of the Cumberland for battle. On December 15, Thomas attacked; he continued attacking the next day; and the Confederate Army of Tennessee broke into pieces. A few fragments reconstituted that army in Tupelo, Mississippi, where Hood, still blaming the luckless soldiers under his command, resigned. Most of the soldiers had deserted and gone home already.

In the winter of 1864 and spring of 1865, desertion nearly destroyed the Confederate army. On New Year's Day 1865, more than half of Confederate soldiers were absent without leave. Desertion drove the Confederate Congress finally to authorize black enlistment, although not emancipation as a reward.

The most potent reason for desertion was the condition of soldiers' families. Letters from home were often pleas for a husband's desertion. To keep such letters out of the soldiers' hands, the Army of Northern Virginia resorted to reading correspondence from home. Sometimes wives and mothers begged husbands and sons to return to protect them from the Yankees, or to help them recover from Yankee devastation. Sometimes, however, families in areas untouched by actual invasion required their men's return because of the high price of food or the difficulty of running farms in their absence. Certainly, Sherman's Georgia Campaign encouraged men to fear for their families.

With no Confederate infantry to oppose it, the 'March to the Sea' was a pleasure walk. Destroying railroads and raiding food and other supplies as it went – in Sherman's phrase, 'smashing things generally' – the army averaged ten miles a day. It reached the outskirts of Savannah, 250 miles from Atlanta, on December 10. Sherman had ordered his army to 'forage liberally' which some soldiers interpreted as a right to loot and destroy. Much of the destruction was of military targets but wrecks of burned down houses and the pocket watches that some soldiers would soon hawk on the streets of Savannah revealed a general failure to distinguish precisely between legitimate and non-legitimate targets. Nonetheless, civilians rarely suffered violence; the march attacked their property and their morale but not their persons. While some soldiers did rape and murder civilians, black and white, most of them restrained themselves in a way that would surprise most people who have come into contact with invading soldiery [29 *vol. II, p. 175*].

Sherman's forces did, by his estimate, $100 million dollars worth of damage to the state of Georgia. Sherman never repented. The people of Georgia had brought the desolation on themselves when they repudiated the government that protected them and appealed to war. As Sherman had earlier told Georgians, 'War is cruelty and you cannot refine it' [*Doc. 11*].

In the beginning of the year, Sherman moved his army into South Carolina, continuing the raid on Confederate logistics that had begun with the 'March to the Sea.' Grant ordered other raids as well. Union forces took Mobile in April. James Harrison Wilson led a large cavalry raid from Tennessee to Selma, Alabama, an industrial and munitions center, and beyond Selma into Georgia where in May he captured Jefferson Davis who was trying to quit the country. Sheridan's troops destroyed much of Richmond's transportation network, including the locks of the James River canal. Sheridan's final raid in late March 1865 broke the Army of Northern Virginia's last supply line.

Before his campaign of the Carolinas, Sherman wrote to Halleck that 'the whole army is burning with an insatiable desire to wreak vengeance upon South Carolina.' Secession began in South Carolina; in the eyes of the soldiers, as well as some Confederate civilians, the state bore a special responsibility for the war. Soldiers burned and looted more there than in Georgia. Sherman's army did not attack Charleston, as many hoped it would, but on February 17, it reached Columbia, the state capital. As they approached the city, some soldiers sang a parody of a patriotic song: 'Hail Columbia, happy land / If I don't burn you, I'll be damned' [28 *p. 5*].

The question of responsibility for the burning of Columbia dates back to the war itself. The most evocative account of the fire is in Charles Royster's *The Destructive War* [28]. Preferring to destroy cotton rather than leave it for the Yankees to capture, the retreating Confederates set bales of cotton on fire. When the army reached the city, some Union soldiers fought the fires, while others deliberately spread them. Liberated prisoners from a near-by POW camp also jubilated in the flames. When the volunteer fire department tried to bring the fires under control, soldiers smashed their firefighting equipment with axes. Gale-force winds spread the fire. Sherman lost control of the army. Some soldiers looted white mansions; others looted slave quarters. One group of soldiers carried a piano into the street, set fire to it and, while one played it the others danced. Drunken soldiers fell asleep in buildings they'd set fire to and died in the flames. A few soldiers stripped, raped and killed African-American women. When Sherman first saw the light of fires, he said, 'They have brought it on themselves.' At three in the morning, he sent in a brigade to restore order. Systematically marching through the city, the brigade shot thirty-two men and arrested 370; patrols eventually arrested 2,500 soldiers and civilians [28].

After the destruction of much of Columbia, Sherman's soldiers acted with restraint. They soon reached North Carolina, a state they judged less harshly as it had been reluctant to secede and supported a strong peace movement. At Bentonsville, the Confederates, again under General Joseph Johnston, attacked one wing of Sherman's army one last time in March 1865; Johnston's men were far too few to stop the Union advance. When two additional Union corps joined Sherman a few days later, Sherman commanded 80,000 men to Johnston's 21,000. Although Johnston squeezed out a few thousand more reinforcements from his department, his principal concern for the remaining days of the war was how to surrender to Sherman. He succeeded at Bennett Place, North Carolina April 26, 1865.

Lee had surrendered the Army of Northern Virginia a few days earlier. Once Sheridan had broken his supply lines, he evacuated the army before Union forces could trap it. He planned to join his army to Johnston's for a last stand against Grant's army and Sherman's. But this time Grant's army moved more quickly than Lee's and blocked the escape route. Lee rejected the proposal of some junior officers that the army disband to conduct a guerilla war, and instead surrendered. When Lee left the private house where the surrender was arranged, some in the Union army began firing celebratory salutes. Grant ordered them stopped. 'The war is over; the rebels are our countrymen again ... ' [10 *vol III, p. 951*].

THE END OF THE WAR

Grant was right, but in some ways he'd spoken too soon. After his meeting with Grant, Lee sent Davis official notification of the surrender; he had surrendered only his army and still recognized Davis as his president. An undeclared war in which the victorious party denies the legitimacy of the opposing government, and a war over so broad a territory as the Confederate States, cannot have one clear-cut moment that ends it. At no one time in April 1865 can it be said that the Confederacy surrendered. Three key events that month represented the end of the war and only one of those was official: the surrender of the Army of Northern Virginia at Appomattox on April 9, 1865, the assassination of Abraham Lincoln on April 14, and the capture of Jefferson Davis on May 10. Nonetheless, the final Confederate surrender did not occur until November 6, when the crew of CSS *Shenandoah*, docking at Liverpool, finally admitted defeat and turned the ship over to the British government.

The war ended with no universal surrender of the Confederate military, let alone of the Confederacy. Since the Union did recognize the Confederate armies as fit subjects for negotiation, Grant encouraged Lee, the Confederate general-in-chief, to surrender all Confederate forces. But Lee, deferring to the authority of the Confederate president, an authority repudiated by the Union, refused. He did surrender the Army of Northern Virginia. The commanders of the other armies in the field followed suit.

Grant practically gave Lee immunity, declaring that the honor of the army protected Lee from arrest. Lee's safe parole made it nearly impossible to arrest any former Confederate for military activities alone. Instead, the federal government, too often through the War Department, arrested high-ranking politicians and Confederates – and their sympathizers – accused of criminal acts. Jefferson Davis was the most important of the former; the so-called Lincoln conspirators an important example of the latter.

Almost immediately after Lee's surrender, John Wilkes Booth, a Marylander sympathetic to the Confederacy and a prominent Shakespearian actor, assassinated Lincoln in a Washington theater. Often dismissed as insane, Booth saw himself as an American Brutus, killing a tyrant at the height of his conquest. Jumping from Lincoln's private box to the theater's stage, Booth delivered his last speech to an audience: 'Sic semper tyrannis.'

Booth was killed resisting capture, but his accomplices were tried by a military court and executed or imprisoned. Executed also were Captain Henry Wirz, commandant of the infamous prison camp at Andersonville, Georgia, and 'Champ' Ferguson, a Confederate guerilla who had murdered black and white Union soldiers after their surrender. Attempts to link Davis personally to Andersonville or Lincoln's assassination failed.

Union cavalry captured Jefferson Davis and his party in Georgia. Davis, who was wearing his wife Varina's shawl, was forever after portrayed in the North dressed as a woman. Imprisoned in Fortress Monroe, Davis accepted the role of Confederate martyr and hoped for his day in court. The federal government declined to bring him to trial and, letting him out on bail, left him in legal limbo the rest of his life, much of which he devoted to telling the world that secession was constitutional and that Joseph Johnston was a poor general.

The fall of Fort Sumter was an oddly bloodless beginning to the bloodiest war in American history; the three military trials immediately after its conclusion were an oddly bloodless end to the largest act of treason in American history. Compare the Hungarian revolt against the Austrians in 1848; the victors of that war executed more than one hundred rebels and imprisoned more than a thousand for twenty years. Some American rebels would be stripped of their right to suffrage and to hold office although even most of them would have their political rights restored in a few years. In general, however, the federal government's postwar policy would operate more directly on the states than on the citizens of the South.

PART THREE ASSESSMENT

CHAPTER EIGHT

EMANCIPATION AND RECONSTRUCTION

EMANCIPATION AS POLICY

Wartime emancipation was the single most revolutionary event in United States history. Even the separation from Great Britain had far fewer immediate social consequences. The long historical moment symbolized by the Emancipation Proclamation but that lasted from January 1, 1863 until the destruction of the Confederacy and the ratification of the Thirteenth Amendment, transformed the United States from the largest slaveholding nation in the world into one officially committed to freedom and free labor but deeply divided on what those concepts meant for those formerly enslaved.

In 1860 the Republican Party had planned to contain slavery; they hoped to abolish it in a generation. Now, far earlier than expected, emancipation had come by the withdrawal of proslavery forces from the national government and by antislavery advocates' opportunistic use of the concept 'military necessity.' Republicans had prepared no master plan for emancipation. Lincoln still entertained the idea of gradual, compensated emancipation in the loyal states and even experimented unsuccessfully with colonization. (The colony, founded on an island off Haiti, proved a disaster.) He believed if African Americans remained in the South, the states should adopt some kind of apprentice system. During the war, Union policy left the freedpeople considerably short of freedom. In many ways, the Reconstruction South might have taken the federal government's policy toward the freedmen as a model for its own.

Winning the war came first; reconstructing the Union second; care and provision for the newly emancipated a distant third. The agency that dealt with the freedpeople most immediately was the Union army, and it was hardly designed with that task in mind. Northern philanthropists also created freedmen's aid societies to help with the transition from slavery to freedom. Furthermore, some businessmen came south simply to take advantage of the economic situation; hiring African Americans, they too participated in developing a pattern for the new post-emancipation South. Finally, the freedpeople tried to achieve what they thought of as true freedom – the opportunity to reunite and protect their families, wage labor, and the independence that came with owning productive property, which they felt years of unpaid work had earned. This last demand was summed up by the phrase 'forty acres and a mule.'

The Union army and navy offered contrabands their first chance to earn wages. Throughout the war the military was the largest employer of African Americans. In general, the military hired former slaves to perform the fatigue duty otherwise done by soldiers and sailors, but too often this was wage labor with no wages. Some in the army believed that the support given to laborers and their families plus emancipation, was all former slaves should have. Even when workers were renumerated, pay was often late to arrive – something that most Union soldiers of all races learned too.

According to the best-informed estimate, at least 474,000 African Americans, the overwhelming majority of them former slaves, worked in some form in the federally-sponsored labor market – as military laborers, agricultural workers, and soldiers. The majority of them worked on plantations. Other freedpeople presumably made private arrangements with landowners or went north for jobs, but we do not know how many.

Willie Lee Rose has written brilliantly about the South Carolina Sea Islands in her *Rehearsal for Reconstruction* [27]. Nowhere else in the occupied South witnessed such deliberate efforts to define the meaning of freedom for the emancipated. The South Carolina Sea Islands, which had come into Union hands early in the war and which had an overwhelming black majority, was the site of the most extensive wartime experimentation with race relations and freedom. The Sea Islands were where the first black regiments were raised. White and black northerners traveled there to establish schools and churches among the freedpeople, while others managed plantations and raised cotton to show that free labor would be profitable and that African Americans would work without the whip. When they discovered that the former slaves rejected growing staple crops and preferred the independence of subsistence farming, they brought black labor into the cotton fields by denying rations.

The Sea Islands, along with Hampton, Virginia and a few other places, stand out. The entire Mississippi Valley was in Union hands by 1863. There the Treasury Department took over running the plantations with very few philanthropic motives. It wanted to make money and used the army to force blacks to sign labor contracts and work for the horde of private businessmen who came down from the North to make a fortune raising cotton. Advocates of northern emigration south argued that they would 'Americanize' the South; and that the South needed 'New Masters' familiar with free labor. What these northern planters wanted was a good crop of cotton and what many supporters of emancipation and free labor sought was a demonstration through a good crop of cotton that African Americans would work outside of slavery. Between them the Treasury Department and the army set up a system halfway between slavery and freedom that could have provided a model for the legislation that the ex-Confederates passed in 1866. The 'free labor market' was one subject not just to economic law but to military regulation [24, 27].

James E. Yeatman of the Western Sanitary Commission reported in 1863 that many freedpeople in the contraband camps and plantations of the Mississippi Valley refused to believe they were free. 'They say they are told they are, but then they are taken and hired to men who treat them, so far as providing for them is concerned, far worse than their "secesh" masters did.' He cited cases of men pressed into government service involuntarily, and of plantation workers receiving neither rations, their proper pay, nor medical attention. Yeatman claimed the majority of men leasing plantations wished only to make a profit: 'they care little whether they make it out of the blood of those they employ or from the soil' [38 *p. 8*].

For those former slaveholders who continued to operate their plantations, this new system was their first experience of 'free labor.' Reluctantly, they learned they could no longer rely on the whip to compel obedience. Freedpeople refused to work the 'dawn-to-dusk' six-day week that had been customary for slaves. The wages mandated by the federal government were low, but they were wages paid by planters for the first time to former slaves. Some military authorities allowed planters to offer their workers a share of the crop at the end of the year in lieu of cash wages, an arrangement favored by many of the freedpeople as well.

A perfect free market in labor exists nowhere and a war zone is an unlikely place to approximate one. Confederate guerillas frequently attacked leased plantations. As Michael Wayne points out, the army wanted to keep the freedpeople on their home plantations in part because of 'the continuingly unstable military condition.' Wayne quotes the general superintendent for freedmen's affairs in the Mississippi Valley, who remembered that 'the problem before us ... was to afford not the best wages to the individual which free competition in an open market might assure him, but a livelihood for the entire population under a condition of military and industrial disorder which temporarily necessitated some form of definite regulation and precluded unrestricted competition' [36 *p. 43*]. The army was not deliberately constructing a model for future labor relations in the South. But willy-nilly, it did. After the war, white southerners would enact so-called black codes, trying to justify them by arguing that a regulated labor market was needed during the transition from slavery to freedom. They would also argue that innate black laziness made it necessary for the law to replace the whip in forcing them to work. Both planters and freed-people would enter the new world of free labor with expectations based on both slavery and the war.

WARTIME RECONSTRUCTION

Historians of the era of sectional conflict conventionally break it into three periods: the coming of the war, the Civil War, and Reconstruction. This is a useful scheme and is the one followed in this book. It is misleading, how-ever, in so far as it suggests that the problems and policies of Recon-struction only began after the close of the war. Whether Reconstruction is defined as the political reintegration of the South into the United States or as the creation of post-emancipation social relations, it practically began as soon as the first Union soldier set foot in the so-called Confederacy.

The question of what would become of the South once it had been conquered or cajoled back into the Union existed before the war even began. What exactly had the seceded states done and did they have a new relationship to the federal government? Republican Congressman Thaddeus Stevens argued that the states had indeed left the Union and that they should be treated as 'conquered provinces,' while Republican Senator Charles Sumner maintained that they had committed suicide and so had returned to their territorial status. Lincoln took a contrary position: as secession was unconstitutional, it had never taken place and the states had never left the Union. The Republican moderates developed a consensus based on Article IV, Section 4 of the Constitution, which guaranteed every state 'a Republican form of government' – that is, non-monarchical. In the light of the 1860s, if not of the 1790s, slaveholding and rebellion had demonstrated that the states of the Confederacy had lost their republican governments and it was a federal responsibility to create new governments. This concept was broad enough to reconcile the idea that the states were still in the Union and the idea that they had gone out.

Another question necessarily unaddressed by the Constitution was which branch of the government would arrange the reintegration of the southern states. Practically speaking, the Supreme Court could be ruled out; both the Republican Congress and the Republican president had been elected on a platform hostile to the Supreme Court, and it would remain a cipher until the 1870s. President Lincoln, who tried to keep all direction of the war in his hands, argued that Reconstruction was his duty. Lincoln based his argument on the presidential pardon power, which could be used to return traitors to citizenship. Since, by his analysis, the 'seceded' states constitutionally had never left the Union, the principal issue was the relationship of a state's citizens and the federal government, not of the state itself. While they were rebels and traitors, they could nonetheless be pardoned by the president.

Congress, more plausibly, claimed Reconstruction as well. By the Constitution, overseeing progress from unorganized territory to organized territory to statehood was a Congressional responsibility and prerogative, and while there was nothing Congress could do if the president insisted on recognizing something as a state, Congress could refuse to seat its senators and representatives. The Republican majority in Congress wanted the ex-Confederate states to be controlled by Unionists and that measures be taken to protect the rights of the freedpeople.

By December 1863, Lincoln believed that the Union army occupied enough of Tennessee, Louisiana, Arkansas, Mississippi, and Virginia for him to begin Reconstruction. He had, among other concerns, his eyes on the autumn 1864 election. His curious schedule for Reconstruction, a proclamation of amnesty based on his pardon powers, became known as the 'ten percent plan' because when ten percent of a state's voters, as measured by the 1860 election, had taken an oath swearing allegiance to the Union and accepting all laws and proclamations concerning slavery, that state could re-establish a state government which Lincoln would recognize. There would be no confiscation of property other than slaves. Lincoln hinted that a reconstructed state government, acknowledging the death of slavery, could and should, 'as a temporary arrangement,' create a special legal status between slavery and freedom for its freedpeople. The abolitionist Wendell Phillips said of Lincoln's plan that it 'frees the slave and ignores the negro' [9 p. 36].

Louisiana was to be the showcase of Lincoln's Reconstruction. Unfortunately, Lincoln and Banks, the Union general administering Louisiana, mishandled the situation. The Unionism of much of New Orleans, which had opposed secession, and the radicalism of its 'free people of color' meant that Louisiana might write and ratify a new state constitution that would permit black suffrage. Lincoln and Banks, however, preferred to trust white Unionists, loyal to the Union but conservative on matters of race. The army's role in the February 1864 election that was intended to restore Louisiana to the Union was heavy-handed; Congress refused to seat Louisiana's representative in 1864, and the representatives of other ex-Confederate states that Lincoln judged reconstructed.

After the February election, Lincoln did hint to the governor of Louisiana that black suffrage, limited to veterans and to the educated, would be advisable. The governor, with prodding from Bank, recommended to the Louisiana constitutional convention that the constitution permit limited black suffrage, leaving the final choice to the state legislature. Nothing came of the proposal.

Congress responded to the ten percent plan with a plan of its own, the Wade–Davis bill that was passed in July 1864. This called for fifty percent of a state's voters to take Lincoln's oath and for delegates to the state convention and future officeholders to take an 'ironclad oath' that they had never voluntarily supported the Confederacy. The Wade–Davis bill also called for special federal courts to protect the rights of freedpeople and for the states to write new constitutions before they could organize a government. Even Congress, however, did not require any form of black suffrage. Representative Henry Winter Davis of Maryland, co-author of the bill, said that making war on the Union had put the rebels outside the Constitution's protection and had given Congress the same authority over them it would have over any defeated enemies.

Unsurprisingly, Lincoln refused to sign a measure that directly repudiated his own formally announced policy. But neither did he veto it and thus return it to Congress where it might be passed over his veto. Instead he pocketed it and proclaimed that any state which preferred to follow the congressional plan could follow it instead of the presidential one. Nobody seriously expected that any state would. Davis and Benjamin Wade responded with an open letter accusing the president – now the nominee of their party – of going beyond his constitutional authority.

But their manifesto did not stop them from campaigning for Lincoln's re-election. Lincoln mended fences as best he could, pushing the Thirteenth Amendment abolishing slavery, appointing Salmon P. Chase Chief Justice of the Supreme Court, supporting a compromise bill that admitted Arkansas and Louisiana, but applied much of the Wade–Davis bill to the rest of the South and that allowed for limited black suffrage. The new Reconstruction bill, however, was not passed, and Lincoln's final word on Reconstruction was a speech he gave from a White House balcony on April 11, 1865 in which he said he wished Louisiana had enfranchised some African Americans, and that he would reveal a new presidential reconstruction policy soon.

Booth's bullet put an end to presidential support for even limited black suffrage. Lincoln's successor, Andrew Johnson, was welcomed by some Radical Republicans as someone who would be sterner toward the former slaveholding class than Lincoln had been; they were unaware of the virulence of Johnson's racism. But what is important to note here is that the issues of Reconstruction were already being debated during the war itself, and that precedents and policies were in place. Fundamental questions – black suffrage, the protection of the freedpeople, congressional or presidential control of the process – were already on the table.

CONSEQUENCES OF THE WAR

The consequences of the Civil War for American history are simultaneously too great to measure and are often exaggerated. Indeed, one may be fairly amused at the sight of historians who study little if anything but the Civil

War announcing it is the single most important event in American history, for we specialists in the field are surely the least likely American historians to know the rest of United States history. There is a tendency to assume that anything that happened after 1865, particularly the vast changes to economic institutions, must be caused by the war. Yet, it is more likely that the war at most accelerated economic change rather than caused it. Surely the two principal results of the war are sufficient to justify any claims made for its centrality to American history.

First, the United States held together. We can only speculate what would have happened had the South succeeded in secession: perhaps two, three or four countries arising from the dismembered United States? American wealth committed as firmly to defense in the nineteenth century as it has been since the Second World War? Slavery lasting into the twentieth century? Novelists, not of a very high order, have written 'might have been' accounts; they rarely show history much changed by Confederate victory and instead insist that the Confederacy would have abolished slavery quickly on its own and that the United States and the Confederate States together would have played the role the United States played in world events in the twentieth century. This vision comes out of an American failure to imagine history as very much different from what it is.

The second result was the social revolution of emancipation. At no other point did so many Americans go through such a change of status. Five million enslaved humans gained their freedom. To contrast, at the time of the American Revolution, there were two and a half million people in the thirteen colonies. Emancipation revolutionized the South. While it has been fashionable to say that, after Reconstruction, southern African Americans were no better off than slaves, such a misapprehension can only be explained by a massive misunderstanding of the nature of legal slavery and the realities of antebellum America.

The fascination of the Civil War, however, lies as much in the experience of the war as the consequences. The American man-of-letters Robert Penn Warren claimed that the Civil War was America's only 'felt' history, 'history lived in the national imagination'. Why this should be remains unclear, but Americans return to the war time and time again. Writing in 1961, Warren concluded that 'we can yet see in the Civil War an image of the powerful, painful, grinding process by which an ideal emerges out of history. That should teach us humility ... but at the same time it draws us to the glory of the human effort to win meaning from the complex and confused motives of men and the blind ruck of event ... And in the contemplation of the story, some of that grandeur, even in the midst of the confused issues, shadowy chances, and brutal ambivalences of our life and historical moment, may rub off on us' [35 *pp. 108–9*].

PART FOUR   DOCUMENTS

Using the American Declaration as a model, the Mississippi Secession Convention argued that northern threats to slavery justified leaving the Union. Other southern secession conventions wrote similar declarations.

A Declaration of the Immediate Causes which Induce and Justify the Secession of the State of Mississippi from the Federal Union.

In the momentous step which our State has taken of dissolving its connection with the government of which we so long formed a part, it is but just that we should declare the prominent reasons which have induced our course.

Our position is thoroughly identified with the institution of slavery – the greatest material interest of the world. Its labor supplies the product which constitutes by far the largest and most important portions of commerce of the earth. These products are peculiar to the climate verging on the tropical regions, and by an imperious law of nature, none but the black race can bear exposure to the tropical sun. These products have become necessities of the world, and a blow at slavery is a blow at commerce and civilization. That blow has been long aimed at the institution, and was at the point of reaching its consummation. There was no choice left us but submission to the mandates of abolition, or a dissolution of the Union, whose principles had been subverted to work out our ruin.

That we do not overstate the dangers to our institution, a reference to a few facts will sufficiently prove.

The hostility to this institution commenced before the adoption of the Constitution, and was manifested in the well-known Ordinance of 1787, in regard to the Northwestern Territory.

The feeling increased, until, in 1819–20, it deprived the South of more than half the vast territory acquired from France.

The same hostility dismembered Texas and seized upon all the territory acquired from Mexico.

It has grown until it denies the right of property in slaves, and refuses protection to that right on the high seas, in the Territories, and wherever the government of the United States had jurisdiction.

It refuses the admission of new slave States into the Union, and seeks to extinguish it by confining it within its present limits, denying the power of expansion.

It tramples the original equality of the South under foot.

It has nullified the Fugitive Slave Law in almost every free State in the Union, and has utterly broken the compact which our fathers pledged their faith to maintain.

It advocates negro equality, socially and politically, and promotes insurrection and incendiarism in our midst.

It has enlisted its press, its pulpit and its schools against us, until the whole popular mind of the North is excited and inflamed with prejudice.

It has made combinations and formed associations to carry out its schemes of emancipation in the States and wherever else slavery exists.

It seeks not to elevate or to support the slave, but to destroy his present condition without providing a better.

It has invaded a State, and invested with the honors of martyrdom the wretch whose purpose was to apply flames to our dwellings, and the weapons of destruction to our lives.

It has broken every compact into which it has entered for our security.

It has given indubitable evidence of its design to ruin our agriculture, to prostrate our industrial pursuits and to destroy our social system.

It knows no relenting or hesitation in its purposes; it stops not in its march of aggression, and leaves us no room to hope for cessation or for pause.

It has recently obtained control of the Government, by the prosecution of its unhallowed schemes, and destroyed the last expectation of living together in friendship and brotherhood.

Utter subjugation awaits us in the Union, if we should consent longer to remain in it. It is not a matter of choice, but of necessity. We must either submit to degradation, and to the loss of property worth four billions of money, or we must secede from the Union framed by our fathers, to secure this as well as every other species of property.

For far less cause than this, our fathers separated from the Crown of England.

Our decision is made. We follow their footsteps. We embrace the alternative of separation; and for the reasons here stated, we resolve to maintain our rights with the full consciousness of the justice of our course, and the undoubting belief of our ability to maintain it.

Journal of the State Convention and Ordinances and Resolutions adopted in January, 1861, with an Appendix. Published by order of the Convention. Jackson, Miss., E. Barksdale, State Printer, 1861.

DOCUMENT 2   **EXCERPTS FROM LINCOLN'S WAR MESSAGE TO CONGRESS**

In the summer of 1861, President Lincoln explained to Congress and thus to the northern people and the world at large, the reasons behind the war, the error of secession, and the nature of a democratic polity.

At the beginning of the present Presidential term, four months ago, the functions of the Federal Government were found to be generally suspended

1. Antietam, MD. President Lincoln with General George B. McClennan and a group of officers.

2. Portrait of Major General Ulysses S. Grant, officer of the Federal Army.

3. Portrait of General Robert E. Lee, officer of the Confederate Army.

4. Fredericksburg, VA. Nurses and officers of the US Sanitary Commission.

5. Cumberland Landing, VA. Group of 'contrabands' at Foller's house.

6. Atlanta, GA. General William T. Sharman, leaning on the breach of a gun, and staff at Federal Fort No.

7. Richmond, VA. Street in the burned district.

8. Gettysburg, PA. Three Confederate prisoners.

within the several States of South Carolina, Georgia, Alabama, Mississippi, Louisiana, and Florida, excepting only those of the Post-Office Department. ...

Simultaneously, and in connection with all this, the purpose to sever the Federal Union was openly avowed. In accordance with this purpose an ordinance had been adopted in each of these States declaring the States, respectively, to be separated from the National Union. A formula for instituting a combined government of these States had been promulgated, and this illegal organization, in the character of Confederate States, was already invoking recognition, aid, and intervention from foreign powers.

Finding this condition of things and believing it to be an imperative duty upon the incoming Executive to prevent, if possible, the consummation of such an attempt to destroy the Federal Union, a choice of means to that end became indispensable. This choice was made and was declared in the inaugural address. The policy chosen looked to the exhaustion of all peaceful measures before a resort to any stronger ones. It sought only to hold the public places and property not already wrested from the Government and to collect the revenue, relying for the rest on time, discussion, and the ballot-box. It promised a continuance of the mails, at Government expense, to the very people who were resisting the Government, and it gave repeated pledges against any disturbance, to any of the people or any of their rights. Of all that which a President might constitutionally and justifiably do in such a case, everything was forborne without which it was believed possible to keep the Government on foot. ...

[Lincoln discusses the Confederate decision to fire upon Fort Sumter and inaugurate war.]

And this issue embraces more than the fate of these United States. It presents to the whole family of man the question whether a constitutional republic or democracy – a Government of the people, by the same people – can or cannot maintain its territorial integrity against its own domestic foes. It presents the question whether discontented individuals, too few in numbers to control administration, according to organic law, in any case, can always, upon the pretenses made in this case, or on any other pretenses, or arbitrarily without any pretense, break up their Government and thus practically put an end to free government upon the earth. It forces us to ask: 'Is there, in all republics, this inherent and fatal weakness?' 'Must a Government, of necessity, be too strong for the liberties of its own people, or too weak to maintain its own existence?' ...

[Lincoln goes on to discuss various war measures, including raising an army and suspension of habeas corpus.]

It is now recommended that you give the legal means for making this contest a short and a decisive one; that you place at the control of the Government for the work at least 400,000 men and $400,000,000. That number of men is about one-tenth of those of proper ages within the regions where apparently all are willing to engage, and the sum is less than a twenty-third part of the money value owned by the men who seem ready to devote the whole. A debt of $600,000,000 now is a less sum per head than was the debt of our Revolution when we came out of that struggle, and the money value in the country now bears even a greater proportion to what it was then than does the population. Surely each man has as strong a motive now to preserve our liberties as each had then to establish them.

A right result now will be worth more to the world than ten times the men and ten times the money. The evidence reaching us from the country leaves no doubt that the material for the work is abundant, and that it needs only the hand of legislation to give it a legal sanction and the hand of the Executive to give it a practical shape and efficiency. One of the greatest perplexities of the Government is to avoid receiving troops faster than it can provide for them. In a word, the people will save their Government if the Government itself will do its part only indifferently well.

It might seem at first thought to be of little difference whether the present movement at the South be called 'secession' or 'rebellion.' The movers, however, well understand the difference. At the beginning they knew they could never raise their treason to any respectable magnitude by any name which implies violation of law. ... They invented an ingenious sophism, which, if conceded, was followed by perfectly logical steps through all the incidents to the complete destruction of the Union. The sophism itself is, that any State of the Union may, consistently with the national Constitution, and therefore lawfully and peacefully, withdraw from the Union without the consent of the Union or of any other State. The little disguise that the supposed right is to be exercised only for just cause, themselves to be the sole judge of its justice, is too thin to merit any notice.

With rebellion thus sugar coated, they have been drugging the public mind of their section for more than thirty years, and until at length they have brought many good men to a willingness to take up arms against the Government the day after some assemblage of men have enacted the farcical pretense of taking their State out of the Union, who could have been brought to no such thing the day before.

This sophism derives much, perhaps the whole, of its currency from the assumption that there is some omnipotent and sacred supremacy pertaining to a State – to each State of our Federal Union. Our States have neither more nor less power than that reserved to them in the Union by the Constitution – no one of them ever having been a State out of the Union. The original ones passed into the Union even before they cast off their

British colonial dependence, and the new ones each came into the Union from a condition of dependence, excepting Texas; and even Texas in its temporary independence was never designated a State. ... Having never been States, either in substance or in name, outside of the Union, whence this magical omnipotence of 'State rights,' asserting a claim of power to lawfully destroy the Union itself. ... The States have their status in the Union, and they have no other legal status. If they break from this they can only do so against law and by revolution. The Union, and not themselves separately, procured their independence and their liberty. ...

This is essentially a people's contest. On the side of the Union it is a struggle for maintaining in the world that form and substance of government whose leading object is to elevate the condition of men; to lift artificial weights from all shoulders; to clear the paths of laudable pursuit for all; to afford all an unfettered start and a fair chance in the race of life. Yielding to partial and temporary departures, from necessity, this is the leading object of the Government for whose existence we contend. I am most happy to believe that the plain people understand and appreciate this. It is worthy of note that while in this, the Government's hour of trial, large numbers of those in the Army and Navy who have been favored with the offices have resigned and proved false to the hand which had pampered them, not one common soldier or common sailor deserted his flag. Great honor is due to those officers who remained true, despite the example of their treacherous associates; but the greatest honor, and most important fact of all, is the unanimous firmness of the common soldiers and common sailors. To the last man, so far as known, they have successfully resisted the traitorous efforts of those whose commands but an hour before they obeyed as absolute law. This is the patriotic instinct of plain people. They understand, without an argument, that the destroying the Government which was made by Washington means no good to them.

Our popular Government has often been called an experiment. Two points in it our people have already settled – the successful establishing and the successful administering of it. One still remains – its successful maintenance against a formidable internal attempt to overthrow it. It is now for them to demonstrate to the world that those who can fairly carry an election can also suppress a rebellion; that ballots are the rightful and peaceful successors of bullets; and that when ballots have fairly and constitutionally decided there can be no successful appeal back to bullets; that there can be no successful appeal except to ballots themselves, at succeeding elections. Such will be a great lesson of peace; teaching men that what they cannot take by an election, neither can they take it by war; teaching all the folly of being the beginners of a war. ...

The Constitution provides, and all States have accepted the provision, that, 'The United States shall guarantee to every State in this Union a republican form of government.' But if a State may lawfully go out of the Union, having done so, it may also discard the republican form of government; so that to prevent its going out is an indispensable means to the end of maintaining the guaranty mentioned; and when an end is lawful and obligatory the indispensable means to it are also lawful and obligatory.

Roy P. Blaser, ed., *The Collected Works of Abraham Lincoln,* Vol. IV, Rutgers University Press, New Brunswick, NJ, 1953, pp. 421–41.

DOCUMENT 3   GENERAL McCLELLAN INSTRUCTS THE PRESIDENT ON THE CONSTITUTION

Despite the retreat of his army before a series of Confederate attacks, Union General McClellan lost none of his self-confidence. The conservative general chose this unlikely moment to lecture President Lincoln on his duties and to warn him against emancipation.

Headquarters, Army of the Potomac, Camp near Harrison's Landing, Va., July 7, 1862.

Mr. President:

You have been fully informed that [the] rebel army is in [our] front, with the purpose of overwhelming us by attacking our positions or reducing us by blocking our river communications. I cannot but regard our condition as critical, and I earnestly desire, in view of possible contingencies, to lay before your excellency, for your private consideration, my general views concerning the existing state of the rebellion, although they do not strictly relate to the situation of this army or strictly come within the scope of my official duties. These views amount to convictions, and are deeply impressed upon my mind and heart. Our cause must never be abandoned; it is the cause of free institutions and self-government. The Constitution and the Union must be preserved, whatever may be the cost in time, treasure, and blood. If secession is successful other dissolutions are clearly to be seen in the future. Let neither military disaster, political faction, nor foreign war shake your settled purpose to enforce the equal operation of the laws of the United States upon the people of every state.

The time has come when the government must determine upon a civil and military policy covering the whole ground of our national trouble.

The responsibility of determining, declaring, and supporting such civil and military policy, and of directing the whole course of national affairs in regard to the rebellion, must now be assumed and exercised by you, or our cause will be lost. The Constitution gives you power sufficient even for the present terrible exigency.

This rebellion has assumed the character of war; as such it should be regarded, and it should be conducted upon the highest principles known to Christian civilization. It should not be a war looking to the subjugation of the people of any State in any event. It should not be at all a war upon population, but against armed forces and political organization. Neither confiscation of property, political executions of persons, territorial organization of States, or forcible abolition of slavery should be contemplated for a moment. In prosecuting the war all private property and unarmed persons should be strictly protected, subject only to the necessity of military operations. All private property taken for military use should be paid or receipted for; pillage and waste should be treated as high crimes; all unnecessary trespass sternly prohibited, and offensive demeanor by the military towards citizens promptly rebuked. Military arrests should not be tolerated, except in places where active hostilities exist, and oaths not required by enactments constitutionally made should be neither demanded nor received. Military government should be confined to the preservation of public order and the protection of political rights. Military power should not be allowed to interfere with the relations of servitude, either by supporting or impairing the authority of the master, except for repressing disorder, as in other cases. Slave contraband under the act of Congress, seeking military protection, should receive it. The right of the Government to appropriate permanently to its own service claims to slave labor should be asserted, and the right of the owner to compensation therefore should be recognized.

This principle might be extended, upon grounds of military necessity and security, to all the slaves within a particular State, thus working manumission in such State; and in Missouri, perhaps in Western Virginia also, and possibly even in Maryland, the expediency of such a measure is only a question of time.

A system of policy thus constitutional and conservative, and pervaded by the influences of Christianity and freedom, would receive the support of almost all truly loyal men, would deeply impress the rebel masses and all foreign nations, and it might be humbly hoped that it would commend itself to the favor of the Almighty.

Unless the principles governing the future conduct of our struggle shall be made known and approved, the effort to obtain requisite forces will be almost hopeless. A declaration of radical views, especially upon slavery, will rapidly disintegrate our present armies. The policy of the government must be supported by concentration of military power. The national forces should not be dispersed in expeditions, posts of occupation, and numerous armies, but should be mainly collected into masses and brought to bear upon the armies of the Confederate States. Those armies thoroughly defeated, the political structure which they support would soon cease to exist. ...

I may be on the brink of eternity; and as I hope forgiveness from my Master, I have written this letter with sincerity towards you and from love of my country.

Geo. B. McClellan

The War of the Rebellion: A Compilation of the Official Records of the Union and
Confederate Armies, Series 1, Vol. 11, Part I, Government Printing Office, Washington, DC,
1880–1901, pp. 73–4.

DOCUMENT 4   **GENERAL LEE PROPOSES AN INVASION TO**
PRESIDENT DAVIS

Precisely because the odds were against the Confederacy, Robert E. Lee
believed that the Conferate army must maintain the initiative and strike
hard at the Union opponents. On September 3 1862, he explained to
President Davis the reasons for the Army of Northern Virginia's Campaign
into Maryland, which would end at the Battle of Antietam.

3d September 1862

The present seems to be the most propitious time, since the commencement of the war, for the Confederate Army to enter Maryland. The two grand armies of the U. S. that have been operating in Virginia, though now united, are much weakened and demoralized. Their new levees, of which, I understand, sixty thousand men have already been posted in Washington, are not yet organized, and will take some time to prepare for the field. If it is ever desired to give material aid to Maryland, and afford her an opportunity of throwing off the oppression to which she is now subject, this would seem the most favorable. After the enemy had disappeared from the vicinity of Fairfax C. H. and taken the road to Alexandria & Washington, I did not think it would be advantageous to follow him further. I had no intention of attacking him in his fortifications, and am not prepared to invest them. If I possessed the necessary munitions, I should be unable to supply provisions for the troops. I therefore determined while threatening the approaches to Washington to draw the troops into Loudon, where forage and some provisions can be obtained, menace their possession of the Shenandoah Valley, and if found practicable, to cross into Maryland.

The purpose, if discovered, will have the effect of carrying the enemy north of the Potomac, and if prevented, will not result in much evil. The army is not properly equipped for an invasion of an enemy's territory. It lacks much of the material of war, is feeble in transportation, the animals being much reduced, and the men [are] poorly provided with clothes, and in thousands of instances, are destitute of shoes. Still we cannot afford to be idle, and though weaker than our opponents in men and military equip ments, must endeavor to harass, if we cannot destroy them. I am aware that the movement is attended with much risk, yet I do not consider success impossible, and shall endeavor to guard it from loss. As long as the army of the enemy are employed on this frontier, I have no fears for the safety of Richmond, yet I earnestly recommend that advantage be taken of this period of comparative safety, to place its defense, both by land and water, in the most perfect condition. A respectable force can be collected to defend its approaches by land, and the steamer Richmond I hope is now ready to clear the river of hostile vessels. Should Gen'l. [Braxton] Bragg find it impracticable to operate to advantage on his present frontier, his army, after leaving sufficient garrisons, could be advantageously employed in opposing the overwhelming numbers which it seems to be the intention of the enemy now to concentrate in Virginia. I have already been told [by] prisoners that some of [Don Carlos] Buell's Cavalry have been joined to Gen'l. [John] Pope's Army, and have reason to believe that the whole of [George B.] McClellan's, the larger portions of [Ambrose E.] Burnside's & [Jacob D.] Coxe's, and a portion of [David] Hunter's, are united to it, what occasions me most concern is the fear of getting out of ammunition. I beg you will instruct the Ordnance Dept. to spare no pains in manufacturing a sufficient amount of the best kind, & to be particular in preparing that for the Artillery, to provide three times as much of the long range ammunition, as of that for smooth bore or short range guns.

The points to which I desire the ammunition to be forwarded, will be made known to the Department in time. If the Qtr. Master's Department [in time] can furnish any shoes, it would be the greatest relief.

We have entered upon September, and the nights are becoming cool.

Haskell Monroe, et al., eds, *The Papers of Jefferson Davis*, Vol. 8, Louisiana State University Press, Baton Rouge, LA and London, 1971–, pp. 373–4.

DOCUMENT 5   AN ANTISLAVERY PETITION SENT TO LINCOLN

As the war continued, more white northerners demanded the abolition of slavery. Lincoln concealed his emancipation policy until after the Battle of Antietam. Consequently, he received petitions such as this, urging him to do what he had already made his mind up to do – strike a blow against southern slavery.

MEMORIAL OF THE PUBLIC MEETING OF THE CHRISTIAN MEN OF CHICAGO.

To His Excellency, Abraham Lincoln, President of the United States:

...

The American nation, in this its judgment-hour, must acknowledge that the cry of the slave, unheeded by man, has been heard by God and answered in this terrible visitation. The time has at length come of which Jefferson solemnly warned his countrymen, as he declared that the slaves of America were enduring 'a bondage, one hour of which is fraught with more misery than ages of that which occasioned the war of the Revolution,' and added, 'When the measure of their tears shall be full, when their tears shall have involved heaven itself in darkness, doubt less a God of justice will awaken to their distress, by diffusing a light and liberality among their oppressors, or at length by his exterminating thunder, manifest his attention to things of this world, and that they are not left to the guidance of blind fatality.'

The slave oligarchy has organized the most unnatural, perfidious and formidable rebellion known to history. It has professedly established an independent government on the avowed basis of slavery, admitting that the Federal Union was constituted to conserve and promote liberty. All but four of the slave states have seceded from the Union, and those four (with the exception of Delaware, in which slavery but nominally exists) have been kept in subjection only by overwhelming military force. Can we doubt that this is a Divine retribution for national sin, in which our crime has justly shaped our punishment?

Proceeding upon this belief, which recent events have made it almost atheism to deny, your memorialists avow their solemn conviction, deepening every hour, that there can be no deliverance from Divine judgments *till slavery ceases in the land*. We cannot expect God to save a nation that clings to its sin. This is too fearful an hour to insult God, or to deceive ourselves. National existence is in peril: our sons and brothers are falling by tens of thousands on the battle-field: the war becomes daily more determined and destructive. While we speak the enemy thunders at the gates of the capital. Our acknowledged superiority of resources has thus far availed little or nothing in the conflict. As Christian patriots we dare not conceal the truth, that these judgments mean what the divine judgments meant in Egypt. They are God's stern command – 'LET MY PEOPLE GO!' ... We urge you, therefore, as the head of this Christian nation, from considerations of moral principle, and, as the only means of preserving the Union, to proclaim, *without delay*, NATIONAL EMANCIPATION.

However void of authority in this respect you might have been in time of peace, you are well aware, as a statesman, that the exigencies of war are the only limits of its powers, especially in a war to preserve the very life of the nation. And these exigencies are not to be restricted to what may avail at the last gasp prior to national death, but are to be interpreted to include all measures that may most readily and thoroughly subdue the enemy. The rebels have brought slavery under your control by their desperate attack upon the life of the republic. They have created a moral, political and military necessity, which warrants the deed, and now God and a waiting world demand that the opportunity be used. And surely the fact that they have placed in our power a system which, while it exposes them, is itself the grossest wickedness, adds infinitely to the obligation to strike the blow. ... Our prayer to God is, that by such an act the name of Abraham LINCOLN may go down to posterity with that of GEORGE WASHINGTON, as the second SAVIOR OF OUR COUNTRY for its overthrow. ...

Memorial of the Public Meeting of the Christian Men of Chicago [Pamphlet], Chicago, *16, 1862*

DOCUMENT 6   **OVER THE CARNAGE ROSE PROPHETIC A VOICE**

The two American poets who struggled most with the meaning of the war were Herman Melville and Walt Whitman. Here Whitman tried to resolve the anomaly of holding together a democratic union by force.

Over the carnage rose prophetic a voice,
Be not dishearten'd – Affection shall solve the problems
of Freedom yet;
Those who love each other shall become invincible –
they shall yet make Columbia victorious.

Sons of the Mother of All! you shall yet be victorious!
You shall yet laugh to scorn the attacks of all the remainder of the earth.

No danger shall balk Columbia's lovers;
If need be, a thousand shall sternly immolate themselves
for one.

One from Massachusetts shall be a Missourian's com-
rade;
From Maine and from hot Carolina, and another an Ore-
gonese, shall be friends triune,
More precious to each other than all the riches of the
earth.

To Michigan, Florida perfumes shall tenderly come:
Not the perfumes of flowers, but sweeter, and wafted
beyond death.
It shall be customary in the houses and streets to see
manly affection;
The most dauntless and rude shall touch face to face
lightly;
The dependence of Liberty shall be lovers,
The continuance of Equality shall be comrades.

These shall tie you and band you stronger than hoops
of iron;
I, extatic, O partners! O lands! with the love of lovers
tie you.
Were you looking to be held together by the lawyers? Or by an
agreement on a paper: or by arms?
–Nay –nor the world, nor any living thing, will so cohere.

Walt Whitman, *Leaves of Grass*, Washington, DC, 1872.

DOCUMENT 7	JEFFERSON DAVIS DISCUSSES THE WAR AND CONFEDERATE POLICY, DECEMBER 1862

In 1862, Davis travelled through the Confederacy in an effort to raise Confederate morale. In his speech to the Mississippi legislature, from which these excerpts are taken, he addressed issues on the homefront, particularly conscription.

You in Mississippi have but little experienced as yet the horrors of the war. You have seen but little of the savage manner in which it is waged by your barbarous enemies. It has been my fortune to witness it in all its terrors; in a part of the country where old men have been torn from their homes, carried into captivity and immured in distant dungeons, and where delicate women have been insulted by a brutal soldiery and forced even to cook for the dirty Yankee invaders; where property has been wantonly destroyed, the country ravaged, and every outrage committed. And it is with these people that our fathers formed a union and a solemn compact. There is indeed a difference between the two peoples. Let no man hug the delusion that there can be renewed association between them. Our enemies are a traditionless and a homeless race; from the time of Cromwell to the present moment they have been disturbers of the peace of the world. Gathered together by Cromwell from the bogs and fens of the North of Ireland and of England, they commenced by disturbing the peace of their own country; they disturbed Holland, to which they fled, and they disturbed England on their return. They persecuted Catholics in England, and they hung Quakers and witches in America. Having been hurried into a war with a people so devoid of every mark of civilization you have no doubt wondered that I have not carried out the policy, which I had intended should be our policy, of fighting our battles on the fields of the enemy instead of suffering him to fight them on ours. This was not the result of my will, but of the power of the enemy. They had at their command all the accumulated wealth of seventy years – the military stores which had been laid up during that time. They had grown rich from the taxes wrung from you for the establishing and supporting their manufacturing institutions. We have entered upon a conflict with a nation contiguous to us in territory, and vastly superior to us in numbers. In the face of these facts the wonder is not that we have done little, but that we have done so much. In the first year of the war our forces were sent into the field poorly armed, and were far inferior in number to the enemy. We were compelled even to arm ourselves by the capture of weapons taken from the foe on the battle-field. Thus in every battle we exchanged our arms for those of the invaders. At the end of twelve months of the war, it was still necessary for us to adopt some expedient to enable us to maintain our ground. The only expedient remaining to us was to call on those brave men who had entered the service of their country at the beginning of the war, supposing that the conflict was to last but a short time, and that they would not be long absent from their homes. The only expedient, I say, was to call on these gallant men; to ask them to maintain their position in front of the enemy, and to surrender for a time their hopes of soon returning to their families and their friends. And nobly did they respond to the call. They answered that they were willing to stay, that they were willing to maintain their position and to breast the tide of invasion. But it was not just that they should stand alone. They asked that the men who had stayed at home – who had thus far been sluggards in the cause – should be forced, likewise, to meet the enemy. From this, resulted the law of Congress, which is known as the conscription act, which declared all men, from the age of eighteen to the age of thirty-five, to be liable to enrollment in the Confederate service. I regret that there has been some prejudice excited against that act, and that it has been subjected to harsher criticism than it deserves. And here I may say that an erroneous impression appears to prevail in regard to this act. It is no disgrace to be brought into the army by conscription. There is no more reason to expect from the citizen voluntary service in the army than to expect voluntary labor on the public roads or the voluntary payment of taxes. But these things we do not expect. We assess the property of the citizen, we appoint tax-gatherers; why should we not likewise distribute equally the labor, and enforce equally the obligation of defending the country from its enemies? I repeat that it is no disgrace to any one to be conscribed, but it is a glory for those who do not wait for the conscription. Thus resulted the conscription act; and thence arose the necessity for the exemption act. That necessity was met; but when it was found that under these acts enough men were not drawn into the ranks of the army to fulfill the purposes intended, it became necessary to pass another exemption act, and another conscription act. It is only of this latter that I desire now to speak. Its policy was to leave at home those men needed to conduct the administration, and those who might be required to support and maintain the industry of the country – in other words, to exempt from military service those whose labor, employed in other avocations, might be more profitable to the country and to the government, than in the ranks of the army.

I am told that this act has excited some discontent and that it has provoked censure, far more severe, I believe, than it deserves. It has been said that it exempts the rich from military service, and forces the poor to fight the battles of the country. The poor do, indeed, fight the battles of the country. It is the poor who save nations and make revolutions. But is it true that in this war the men of property have shrunk from the ordeal of the battle-field? Look through the army; cast your eyes upon the maimed heroes of the war whom you meet in your streets and in the hospitals; remember the martyrs of the conflict; and I am sure you will find among them more than a fair proportion drawn from the ranks of men of property. The object of that portion of the act which exempts those having charge of twenty or more negroes, was not to draw any distinction of classes, but simply to provide a force, in the nature of a police force, sufficient to keep our negroes in control. This was the sole object of the clause. Had it been otherwise, it would never have received my signature. As I have already said, we have no cause to complain of the rich. All of our people have done well; and, while the poor have nobly discharged their duties, most of the wealthiest and most distinguished families of the South have representatives in the ranks. ...

Permit me now to say that I have seen with peculiar pleasure the recommendation of your Governor in his message, to make some provision for the families of the absent soldiers of Mississippi. Let this provision be made for the objects of his affection and his solicitude, and the soldier engaged in fighting the battles of his country will no longer be disturbed in his slumber by dreams of an unprotected and neglected family at home. Let him know that his mother Mississippi has spread her protecting mantle over those he loves, and he will be ready to fight your battles, to protect your honor, and, in your cause, to die. ...

The exemption act, passed by the last Congress, will probably be made the subject of revision and amendment. It seems to me that some provision might be made by which those who are exempt from enrollment now, might, on becoming subject to conscription, be turned over by the State to the Confederate authorities. But let it never be said that there is a conflict between the States and the Confederate government, by which a blow may be inflicted on the common cause. If such a page is to be written on the history of any State, I hope that you, my friends, will say that that State shall not be Mississippi. ...

I may say here that I did not expect the Confederate enrolling officers to carry on the work of conscription. I relied for this upon the aid of the State authorities. I supposed that State officers would enroll the conscripts within the limits of their respective States, and that Confederate officers would then receive them in camps of instruction. This I believe to be the policy of your Governor's arguments. We cannot too strongly enforce the necessity of harmony between the Confederate Government and the State Governments. They must act together if our cause is to be brought to a successful issue. Of this you may rest assured, whatever the Confederate government can do for the defense of Mississippi will be done. I feel equal confidence that whatever Mississippi can do will likewise be done. It undoubtedly requires legislation to cause men to perform those duties which are purely legal. Men are not apt to feel an obligation to discharge duties from which they may have been exempted. Ours is a representative government, and it is only through the operation of the law that the obligations toward it can be equally distributed. When the last Congress proclaimed that a certain number of men were required to fill up the ranks of the army, that class of men who were already in the field and who were retained in service, would not have been satisfied had there been no conscription of those who had remained at home. I may state also, that I believe this to be the true theory for the military defense of the Confederacy. Cast your eyes forward to that time at the end of the war, when peace shall nominally be proclaimed – for peace between us and our hated enemy will be liable to be broken at short intervals for many years to come – cast your eyes forward to that time, and you will see the necessity for continued preparation and unceasing watchfulness. We have but few men in our country who will be willing to enlist in the army for a soldier's pay. But if every young man shall have served for two or three years in the army, he will be prepared when war comes to go into camp and take his place in the ranks an educated and disciplined soldier. Serving among his equals, his friends and his neighbors, he will find in the army no distinction of class. To such a system I am sure there can be no objection.

The issue before us is one of no ordinary character. We are not engaged in a conflict for conquest, or for aggrandizement, or for the settlement of a point of international law. The question for you to decide is, 'will you be slaves or will you be independent?' Will you transmit to your children the freedom and equality which your fathers transmitted to you or will you bow down in adoration before an idol baser than ever was worshipped by Eastern idolaters? Nothing more is necessary than the mere statement of this issue. Whatever may be the personal sacrifices involved, I am sure that you will not shrink from them whenever the question comes before you. Those men who now assail us, who have been associated with us in a common Union, who have inherited a government which they claim to be the best the world ever saw – these men, when left to themselves, have shown that they are incapable of preserving their own personal liberty. They have destroyed the freedom of the press; they have seized upon and imprisoned members of State Legislatures and of municipal councils, who were suspected of sympathy with the South. Men have been carried off into captivity in distant States without indictment, without a knowledge of the accusations brought against them, in utter defiance of all rights guaranteed by the institutions under which they live. These people, when separated from the South and left entirely to themselves, have, in six months, demonstrated their utter incapacity for self-government. And yet these are the people who claim to be your masters. These are the people who have determined to divide out the South among their Yankee troops. Mississippi they have devoted to the direst vengeance of all. 'But vengeance is the Lord's,' and beneath his banner you will meet and hurl back these worse than vandal hordes.

The great end and aim of the government is to make our struggle successful. The men who stand highest in this contest would fall the first sacrifice to the vengeance of the enemy in case we should be unsuccessful. You may rest assured then for that reason if for no other that whatever capacity they possess will be devoted to securing the independence of the country. Our government is not like the monarchies of the Old World, resting for support upon armies and navies. It sprang from the people and the confidence of the people is necessary for its success. ...

In the course of this war our eyes have been often turned abroad. We have expected sometimes recognition and sometimes intervention at the hands of foreign nations, and we have had a right to expect it. Never before in the history of the world had a people for so long a time maintained their ground, and showed themselves capable of maintaining their national existence, without securing the recognition of commercial nations. I know not why this has been so, but this I say, 'put not your trust in princes,' and rest not your hopes in foreign nations. This war is ours; we must fight it out ourselves, and I feel some pride in knowing that so far we have done it without the good will of anybody. ...

I can then say with confidence that our condition is in every respect greatly improved over what it was last year. Our armies have been augmented, our troops have been instructed and disciplined. The articles necessary for the support of our troops, and our people, and from which the enemy's blockade has cut us off, are being produced in the Confederacy. Our manufactories have made rapid progress, so much is this the case that I learn with equal surprise and pleasure from the general commanding this department, that Mississippi alone can supply the army which is upon her soil.

Our people have learned to economize and are satisfied to wear home spun. I never see a woman dressed in home spun that I do not feel like taking off my hat to her; and although our women never lose their good looks, I cannot help thinking that they are improved by this garb. I never meet a man dressed in home spun but I feel like saluting him. I cannot avoid remarking with how much pleasure I have noticed the superior morality of our troops, and the contrast which in this respect they present to those of the invader. I can truly say that an army more pious and more moral than that defending our liberties, I do not believe to exist. On their valor and the assistance of God I confidently rely.

Haskell Monroe, et al., eds, *The Papers of Jefferson Davis*, Vol. 8, pp. 565–79.

DOCUMENT 8   PLANTING, SLAVES AND THE WAR:
MARY JANE BRASFIELD LIPSCOMB TO JEFFERSON DAVIS

War and the 1862 Confederate Conscription Act took men away from their homes. This disrupted the southern homefront and caused particular fears for a society based on racial slavery. In November 1862, after Lincoln's first Emancipation Proclamation, a southern white woman wrote to her president to ask that her husband be sent home to discipline her family's slaves.

Forkland Green County Ala. 15th Nov/62.

...

I am the wife of Joel Q. Lipscomb now a Soldier in the Confederate service. 1 st Battalion Alabama, Artillery. Immediately upon the passage of the Conscript law – before any exemptions were made known, and under the impression that he would be compelled to go into the service at any sacrifice he proceeded to Mobile and entered the service under Gen. [John H.] Forney – where he is now stationed.

We have a farm in Choctaw County, Alabama with over forty negroes thereon, now entirely without a superintendent, negroes running at large, with the usual confusion and destruction in such cases, and your Excellency must be aware of the fact, that through the agency of the Conscript law, the male population of the country has been taken away, hence the utter impossibility of procuring an overseer or superintendent at all reliable.

I have been compelled to leave my home in Choctaw County and come here to reside temporarily with my Father until some one could be had to control our slaves. Thus your Excellency will see that I am eighty miles from my home – our farm and negroes, like a ship without sail or rudder, that a general wreck and destruction must ensue without relief. I have sought in vain for aid. I addressed a Petition to the Hon. Secretary of War setting forth all these facts; that officer has not found time to answer in any shape, and I am left the only and last alternative of appealing to both the Justice and magnanimity of the Government to afford relief before irreparable ruin overtakes us, and I know of no other avenue now, through which to approach the Government, but to go directly to its Head who controls the temporal destiny of us all – I therefore ask that an order be issued from the proper authorities directed to the proper Military officer that my said husband be detailed set-apart or exempted under the Conscript law to take charge of our said farm and negroes as the produce raised upon said farm under proper management will be worth much more to the country than the Services of individual. ...

Your Excellency is doubtless in constant attention to the ponderous business of the Government with that undying solicitude that could alone be upheld by a love of Freedom Constitutional liberty and the great principles of self Government yet I hope your Excellency will find time enough amidst all this, to give me a hearing and grant me the relief sought for.

Very Respectfully.
Mary Jane Lipscomb.

N.B. It is thought by many that we will have trouble here about Christmas holidays, with our slaves, growing out of the *Emancipation Proclamation* of the *Lincoln* Government

Haskell Monroe, et al., eds, *The Papers of Jefferson Davis*, Vol. 8, pp. 493–4.

DOCUMENT 9   U. S. GRANT ON THE MILITARY SITUATION IN SPRING 1864

The promotion of General Grant to overall command of the Union army finally unified the Union high command and created a broad and ultimately successful military strategy. In these passages, Grant discussed the military situation as it existed soon after he took command. In the first two, which come from Grant's memoirs, he explained Lincoln's attitude toward him and his overall strategy. In the last, from a letter written in 1864, Grant warned Sherman to keep on the offensive.

(a) From his memoirs
In my first interview with Mr. Lincoln alone he stated to me that he had never professed to be a military man or to know how campaigns should be conducted, and never wanted to interfere in them: but that procrastination on the part of commanders, and the pressure from the people at the North and Congress, *which was always with him*, forced him into issuing his series of 'Military Orders' – one, two, three, etc. He did not know but they were all wrong, and did know that some of them were. All he wanted or had ever wanted was some one who would take the responsibility and act, and call him for all the assistance needed, pledging himself to use all the power of the government in rendering such assistance. Assuring him that I would do the best I could with the means at hand, and avoid as far as possible annoying him or the War Department our first interview ended. ...

The armies were now all ready to move for the accomplishment of a single object. They were acting as a unit so far as such a thing was possible over such a vast field. Lee, with the capital of the Confederacy, was the main end to which all were working. Johnston, with Atlanta, was an important obstacle in the way of our accomplishing the result aimed at, and was therefore almost an independent objective. It was of less importance only because the capture of Johnston and his army would not produce so immediate and decisive a result in closing the rebellion as would the possession of Richmond, Lee and his army. All other troops were employed exclusively in support of these two movements. This was the plan. ...

Ulysses S. Grant, *Memoirs and Selected Letters*, Library of America, New York, 1990, pp. 473, 489.

(b) From a letter to Sherman

What I now want more particularly to say is, that if the two main attacks, yours and the one from here, should promise great success the enemy may in a fit of desperation, abandon one part of their line of defense and throw their whole strength upon a single army, believing that a defeat with one victory to sustain them better than a defeat all along their line, and hoping too at the same time that the army meeting with no resistance will rest perfectly satisfied with their laurels having penetrated to a given point south thereby enabling them to throw their force first upon one and then on the other.

With the majority of Military commanders they might do this. But you have had too much experience in traveling light and subsisting upon the country to be caught by any such ruse. I hope my experience has not been thrown away. My directions then would be if the enemy in your front show signs of joining Lee follow him up to the full extent of your ability. I will prevent the concentration of Lee upon your front if it is in the power of this Army to do it.

The War of the Rebellion: A Compilation of the Official Records of the Union and Confederate Armies, Series I, Vol. 32, Part III, p. 409.

DOCUMENT 10 **DEMOCRATIC AND REPUBLICAN PRESIDENTIAL PLATFORMS**

The 1864 presidential election was fiercely contested, even though the party in power would win with a huge majority. While actually campaigning, Democrats engaged in race-baiting. Their platform, however, focused on war-weariness and civil liberties. Despite their call for a peace conference, the Democrats still insisted that they sought restoration of the Union.

(a) Democratic

August 29, 1864

Resolved, That this Convention does explicitly declare, as the sense of the American people, that after four years of failure to restore the Union by the experiment of war, during which, under the pretense of a military necessity, or war power higher than the Constitution, the Constitution itself has been disregarded in every part, and public liberty and private right alike trodden down and the material prosperity of the country essentially impaired – justice, humanity, liberty, and the public welfare demand that immediate efforts be made for a cessation of hostilities, with a view to an ultimate Convention of the States, or other peaceable means, to the end that at the earliest practicable moment peace may be restored on the basis of the Federal Union of the States.

Resolved, That the direct interference of the military authorities of the United States in the recent elections held in Kentucky, Maryland, Missouri, and Delaware, was a shameful violation of the Constitution; and a repetition of such acts in the approaching election will be held as revolutionary, and will be resisted with all the means and power under our control.

Resolved, That the aim and object of the Democratic Party is to preserve the Federal Union and the rights of the States unimpaired; and they hereby declare that they consider that the administrative usurpation of extraordinary and dangerous powers not granted by the Constitution; the subversion of the civil by the military law in States not in insurrection; the arbitrary arrest, imprisonment, trial, and sentence of American citizens in States where civil law exists in full force; the suppression of freedom of speech and of the press; the denial of the right of asylum; the open and avowed disregard of State rights; the employment of unusual test-oaths, and the interference with and denial of the right of the people to bear arms in their defense, is calculated to prevent a restoration of the Union and the perpetuation of a Government deriving its just powers from the consent of the governed.

(b) Republican (Union)

The Republican platform was broader than that of the Democrats. Republicans urged a continuation of the war, identified Union soldiers, sailors and Lincoln as heroes, and, distinguishing slavery as the greatest threat to Union, proposed its abolition north and south.

1. Resolved, That it is the highest duty of every American citizen to maintain against all their enemies the integrity of the Union and the paramount authority of the Constitution and laws of the United States; and that, laying aside all differences of political opinion, we pledge ourselves, as Union men, animated by a common sentiment and aiming at a common object, to do everything in our power to aid the Government in quelling by force of arms the Rebellion now raging against its authority, and in bringing to the punishment due to their crimes the Rebels and traitors arrayed against it.

2. Resolved, That we approve the determination of the Government of the

United States not to compromise with Rebels, or to offer them any terms of peace, except such as may be based upon an unconditional surrender of their hostility and a return to their just allegiance to the Constitution and laws of the United States, and that we call upon the Government to maintain this position and to prosecute the war with the utmost possible vigor to the complete suppression of the Rebellion, in full reliance upon the self-sacrificing patriotism, the heroic valor and the undying devotion of the American people to the country and its free institutions.

3. Resolved, That as slavery was the cause, and now constitutes the strength of this Rebellion, and as it must be, always and everywhere, hostile to the principles of Republican Government, justice and the National safety demand its utter and complete extirpation from the soil of the Republic; and that, while we uphold and maintain the acts and proclamations by which the Government, in its own defense, has aimed a deathblow at this gigantic evil, we are in favor, furthermore, of such an amendment to the Constitution, to be made by the people in conformity with its provisions, as shall terminate and forever prohibit the existence of Slavery within the limits of the jurisdiction of the United States.

4. Resolved, That the thanks of the American people are due to the soldiers and sailors of the Army and Navy, who have periled their lives in defense of the country and in vindication of the honor of its flag; that the nation owes to them some permanent recognition of their patriotism and their valor, and ample and permanent provision for those of their survivors who have received disabling and honorable wounds in the service of the country; and that the memories of those who have fallen in its defense shall be held in grateful and everlasting remembrance.

5. Resolved, That we approve and applaud the practical wisdom, the unselfish patriotism and the unswerving fidelity to the Constitution and the principles of American liberty, with which ABRAHAM LINCOLN has discharged, under circumstances of unparalleled difficulty, the great duties and responsibilities of the Presidential office; that we approve and endorse, as demanded by the emergency and essential to the preservation of the nation and as within the provisions of the Constitution, the measures and acts which he has adopted to defend the nation against its open and secret foes; that we approve, especially, the Proclamation of Emancipation, and the employment as Union soldiers of men heretofore held in slavery; and that we have full confidence in his determination to carry these and all other Constitutional measures essential to the salvation of the country into full and complete effect.

6. Resolved, That we deem it essential to the general welfare that harmony should prevail in the National Councils, and we regard as worthy of public confidence and official trust those only who cordially endorse the principles proclaimed in these resolutions, and which should characterize the administration of the government.

7. Resolved, That the Government owes to all men employed in its armies, without regard to distinction of color, the full protection of the laws of war – and that any violation of these laws, or of the usages of civilized nations in time of war, by the Rebels now in arms, should be made the subject of prompt and full redress.

8. Resolved, That foreign immigration, which in the past has added so much to the wealth, development of resources and increase of power to the nation, the asylum of the oppressed of all nations, should be fostered and encouraged by a liberal and just policy.

9. Resolved, That we are in favor of the speedy construction of the railroad to the Pacific coast.

10. Resolved, That the National faith, pledged for the redemption of the public debt, must be kept inviolate, and that for this purpose we recommend economy and rigid responsibility in the public expenditures, and a vigorous and just system of taxation; and that it is the duty of every loyal state to sustain the credit and promote the use of the National currency.

11. Resolved, That we approve the position taken by the Government that the people of the United States can never regard with indifference the attempt of any European Power to overthrow by force or to supplant by fraud the institutions of any Republican Government on the Western Continent and that they will view with extreme jealousy, as menacing to the peace and independence of their own country, the efforts of any such power to obtain new footholds for Monarchical Government, sustained by foreign military force, in near proximity to the United States.

Edmund McPherson, *The Political History of the United States of America during the Great Rebellion*, Philp and Solomons, Washington, DC, 1865, pp. 403–7, 417–20.

DOCUMENT 11   **ATLANTANS AND SHERMAN DISCUSS THE NATURE OF WAR**

After the capture of Atlanta, Sherman ordered its civilian population to be evacuated. The mayor and city council complained to the general about what they saw as his needless cruelty. Sherman responded with a lecture on the meaning of war, in particular this civil war.

ATLANTA, Ga., Sept. 11, 1864.
Sir: The undersigned, Mayor and two members of Council for the city of Atlanta, for the time being the only legal organ of the people of said city to express their wants and wishes, ask leave most earnestly but respectfully to petition you to reconsider the order requiring them to leave Atlanta. At first view, it struck us that the measure would involve extraordinary hardship

and loss, but since we have seen the practical execution of it, so far as it has progressed, and the individual condition of many of the people, and heard the statements as to the inconvenience, loss and suffering attending it, we are satisfied that the amount of it will involve in the aggregate consequences appalling and heart-rending.

Many poor women are in an advanced state of pregnancy; others having young children, whose husbands, for the greater part, are either in the army, prisoners, or dead. Some say: 'I have such a one sick at my house; who will wait on them when I am gone?' Others say: 'what are we to do; we have no houses to go to, and no means to buy, build, or rent any; no parents, relatives or friends to go to.' Another says: 'I will try and take this or that article of property; but such and such things I must leave behind, though I need them much.' We reply to them: 'Gen. Sherman will carry your property to Rough and Ready, and then Gen. Hood will take it thence on;' and they will reply to that: 'But I want to leave the railroad at such a place, and cannot get conveyance from thence on.'

We only refer to a few facts to illustrate, in part, how this measure will operate in practice. As you advanced, the people north of us fell back, and before your arrival here a large portion of the people here had retired south; so that the country south of this is already crowded, and without sufficient houses to accommodate the people, and we are informed that many are now staying in churches and other outbuildings. This being so, how is it possible for the people still here (mostly women and children) to find shelter, and how can they live through the winter in the woods; no shelter or subsistence; in the midst of strangers who know them not, and without the power to assist them much if they were willing to do so?

This is but a feeble picture of the consequences of this measure. You know the woe, the horror, and the suffering cannot be described by words. Imagination can only conceive to it, and we ask you to take these things into consideration. We know your mind and time are continually occupied with the duties of your command, which almost deters us from asking your attention to the matter, but thought it might be that you had not considered the subject in all of its awful consequences, and that, on reflection, you, we hope, would not make this people an exception to all mankind, for we know of no such instance ever having occurred – surely not in the United States. And what has this helpless people done that they should be driven from their homes, to wander as strangers, outcasts and exiles, and to subsist on charity?

...

Respectfully submitted,
JAMES M. CALHOUN, Mayor E.E. RAWSON, S.C. WELLS, Councilmen.

GENERAL SHERMAN'S REPLY

Gentlemen: I have your letter of the 11th, in the nature of a petition to re-voke my orders removing all the inhabitants from Atlanta. I have read it carefully, and give full credit to your statements of the distress that will be occasioned by it, and yet shall not revoke my order, simply because my orders are not designed to meet the humanities of the ease, but to prepare for the future struggles, in which millions, yea hundreds of millions of good people outside of Atlanta have a deep interest. We must have *Peace*, not only at Atlanta, but in all America. To secure this, we must stop the war that now desolates our once happy and favored country. To stop war we must defeat the Rebel armies that are arrayed against the laws and Constitution which all must respect and obey. To defeat these armies we must prepare the way to reach them in their recesses, provided with the arms and instruments which enable us to accomplish our purpose.

Now, I know the vindictive nature of our enemy, and that we may have many years of military operations from this quarter, and therefore deem it wise and prudent to prepare in time. The use of Atlanta for warlike purposes is inconsistent with its character as a home for families. There will be no manufactures, commerce or agriculture here for the maintenance of families, and sooner or later want will compel the inhabitants to go. Why not go *now*, when all the arrangements are completed for the transfer, instead of waiting till the plunging shot of contending armies will renew the scene of the past month? Of course I do not apprehend any such thing at this moment, but you do not suppose that this army will be here till the war is over. I cannot discuss this subject with you fairly, because I cannot impart to you what I propose to do, but I assert that my military plans make it necessary for the inhabitants to go away, and I can only renew my offer of services to make their exodus in any direction as easy and comfortable as possible. You cannot qualify war in harsher terms than I will.

War is cruelty, and you cannot refine it; and those who brought war on the country deserve all the curses and maledictions a people can pour out. I know I had no hand in making this war, and I know I will make more sacrifices to-day than any of you to secure peace. But you cannot have peace and a division of our country. If the United States submits to a division now, it will not stop, but will go on until we reap the fate of Mexico, which is eternal war. The United States does and must assert its authority wherever it has power; if it relaxes one bit to pressure it is gone, and I know that such is not the national feeling. This feeling assumes various shapes, but always comes back to that of *Union*. Once admit the Union, once more acknowledge the authority of the National Government, and instead of devoting your houses and streets and roads to the dread uses of war, I, and this army, become at once your protectors and supporters, shielding you from danger, let it come from what quarters it may. I know that a few individuals cannot resist a torrent of error and passion such as has swept the South into rebellion; but you can point out, so that we may know those who desire a Government and those who insist on war and its desolation.

You might as well appeal against the thunderstorm as against these terrible hardships of war. They are inevitable, and the only way the people of Atlanta can hope once more to live in peace and quiet at home is to stop this war which can alone be done by admitting that it began in error and is perpetuated in pride. We don't want your negroes or your horses, or your houses or your land, or anything you have; but we do want and will have a just obedience to the laws of the United States. ... I myself have seen in Missouri, Kentucky, Tennessee, and Mississippi, hundreds and thousands of women and children fleeing from your armies and desperadoes, hungry and with bleeding feet. In Memphis, Vicksburg, and Mississippi we fed thousands upon thousands of the families of rebel soldiers left on our hands, and whom we could not see starve. Now that war comes home to you, you feel very different – you deprecate its horrors, but did not feel them when you sent car-loads of soldiers and ammunition and molded shell and shot to carry war into Kentucky and Tennessee, and desolate the homes of hundreds and thousands of good people, who only asked to live in peace at their old homes, and under the government of their inheritance. But these comparisons are idle. I want peace, and believe it can only be reached through Union and war, and I will ever conduct war purely with a view to perfect and early success. ...

William T. Sherman, *Memoirs of General William T. Sherman*, Vol. 2, Indiana Univesity Press, Bloomington, IN, 1957, pp. 124–7.

CHRONOLOGY

1860

Autumn   Abraham Lincoln elected president.

	Electoral vote	Popular vote
Lincoln	180	1,866,452
Douglas	12	1,376,957
Breckinridge	72	849,781
Bell	39	588,879

20 December   Secession of South Carolina.

1861

9 January   Secession of Mississippi.

10 January   Secession of Florida

11 January   Secession of Alabama.

19 January   Secession of Georgia.

26 January   Secession of Louisiana.

29 January   The State of Kansas is admitted to the Union.

1 February   Secession of Texas.

4 February   Delegates from seceded states meet at Montgomery, Alabama, to form the Confederate States of America.

13 February   Virginia secession convention begins deliberations.

4 March   Inauguration of Abraham Lincoln as president.

4 April   Virginia convention votes down secession.

14 April   Surrender of Fort Sumter to Confederate forces.

17 April   Secession of Virginia.

7 May   Secession of Tennessee and Arkansas.

20 May   Secession of North Carolina.

21 July   First Battle of Bull Run.

Union army: 33,000; casualties, 2,896.

Confederate army: 32,000; casualties, 1,982.

7 November   Capture of Hilton Head, Port Royal, and St Helena Islands, South Carolina.

1862

6 February	Fort Henry on the Tennessee River surrenders to Union naval forces.
8 February	Capture of Roanoke Island, NC by Union forces.
16 February	Fort Donelson on the Cumberland River surrenders.
23 February	Nashville surrenders.
7–8 March	Battle of Pea Ridge.
8–9 March	Battle of Hampton Roads. An indecisive naval battle, notable as the first in the war in which ironclad ships, the *CSS. Virginia* and the *USS Monitor*, fight one another.
17 March	McClellan begins transfer of the Army of the Potomac to the Peninsula.
6–7 April	Battle of Shiloh.
	Union army: 75,000 [note, Grant begins battle with 39,000; 36,000 additional soldiers under Buell arrive the night of April 6]; casualties, 13,047.
	Confederate army: 44,000; casualties, 10,694.
14 April	Congress approves the District Emancipation Act, ending slavery in Washington, DC.
31 May–1 June	Battle of Seven Pines.
	Union army: 42,000; casualties, 5,031.
	Confederate army: 42,000; casualties, 6,134.
25 June–1 July	Seven Days' Battle.
	Union army: 100,000; casualties, 15,849.
	Confederate army: 90,000; casualties, 20,141.
16 July	Congress approves the Second Confiscation Act.
22 July	Lincoln announces Emancipation Proclamation to his Cabinet.
29–30 August	Second Battle of Bull Run.
	Union army: 60,000; casualties, 16,000.
	Confederate army: 50,000; casualties, 9,200.
17 September	Battle of Antietam.
	Union army: 75,000; casualties, 11,350.
	Confederate army: 40,000; casualties, 11,850.
22 September	Preliminary Emancipation Proclamation.
8 October	Battle of Perryville.
8 November	*USS San Jacinto* stops the British ship *Trent* and seizes Confederate diplomats James M. Mason and John Slidell, creating an international incident.

13 December	Battle of Fredericksburg.
	Union army: 130,000; casualties, 12,653.
	Confederate army: 75,000; casualties, 5,309.
31 December– 2 January 1863	Battle of Murfreesboro.
	Union army: 42,000; casualties, 13,249.
	Confederate army: 36,000; casualties, 10,226.

1863

1 January	Final Emancipation Proclamation.
1–4 May	Battle of Chancellorsville.
	Union army: 115,000; casualties, 17,000.
	Confederate army: 60,000; casualties, 13,000.
5 May	The arrest of Ohio Peace Democrat Clement Vallandigham by Union army; on 26 May Vallandigham was banished to the Confederacy.
11 June	Vallandigham is nominated as Democratic gubernatorial candidate.
20 June	State of West Virginia is admitted to the Union.
1–3 July	Battle of Gettysburg.
	Union army: 86,000; casualties, 23,049.
	Confederate army: 75,000; casualties, 25,000.
July 4	Surrender of Vicksburg.
11–13 July	New York City Draft Riots.
19–20 September	Battle of Chickamauga.
	Union army: 58,000; casualties, 16,170.
	Confederate army: 66,000; casualties, 18,454.
23–25 November	Battle of Chattanooga.
	Union army: 60,000; casualties, 5,825.
	Confederate army: 40,000; casualties, 6,600.

1864

12 April	Fort Pillow Massacre.
5–7 May	Battle of the Wilderness.
	Union army: 115,000; casualties, 17,500.
	Confederate army: 60,000; casualties, 7,500,
1–3 June	Battle of Cold Harbor.
27 June	Battle of Kennesaw Mountain.
22 July	Battle of Atlanta.
23 June–12 July	Early's Washington Raid.

30 July	Battle of the Crater (Petersburg, Virginia).
5 August	Naval battle at Mobile Bay.
Autumn	Lincoln is re-elected.

	Electoral vote	Popular vote
Lincoln	212	2,206,938
McClellan	21	1,803,787

12 October	Death of Supreme Court Chief Justice Roger B. Taney.
31 October	The State of Nevada is admitted to the Union.
15 November	Sherman's army begins its 'March to the Sea'.
30 November	Battle of Franklin.
	Union army: 28,000; casualties, 2,326.
	Confederate army: 39,000; casualties, 6,200.
15–16 December	Battle of Nashville.
	Union army: 70,000; casualties, 3,000.
	Confederate army: 33,000; casualties, 6,000.

1865

31 January	Congress passes the Thirteenth Amendment, abolishing slavery. (Final ratification, December 18 1865.)
17 February	The Army of the Tennessee occupies Columbia, South Carolina.
19-21 March	Battle of Bentonsville.
2 April	Selma, Alabama, Confederate munitions center, is captured by Union cavalry.
9 April	The Army of Northern Virginia surrenders.
15 April	Lincoln is assassinated.
26 April	Joseph E. Johnston's army surrenders.
4 May	Richard Taylor's army surrenders.
10 May	Union cavalry captures Jefferson Davis.
12–13 May	Battle of Palmetto Ranch.
26 May	Kirby Smith's army surrenders.
23 June	Brigadier General and Cherokee Chief Stand Watie surrender.
6 November	*CSS. Shenandoah* surrenders.

GLOSSARY

Abolition Abolitionists are distinguished from the American antislavery movements that came before by their demand for an immediate rather than a gradual
end to slavery. Abolitionism had many internal divisions, the most important
being between William Lloyd Garrison and his followers, who rejected politics
and relied on 'moral suasion,' and political abolitionists such as those in the
Liberty Party.

Army Two or more corps. Formally, the largest unit in both the Confederate and
Union armies; however, later in the war generals commanded what are now
called army groups.

Black Belt An extremely fertile agricultural region in the American South, stretch-
ing from Georgia across Alabama and into Mississippi. The Black Belt was
named for the dark color of its soil, not for its large African-American
population, but since most farm land in the Black Belt was owned by plantation
owners, the Black Belt indeed saw a concentration of black slaves.

Border states The four slave states, Delaware, Maryland, Kentucky, and Missouri.

Brigade A brigade is generally considered to be four to six regiments of either
cavalry or infantry, and was, in theory, commanded by a brigadier general, but in
practise was often commanded by the senior colonel.

Casualties The killed, missing, and wounded.

Company Practically speaking, the smallest military unit: one hundred soldiers
commanded by a captain. Companies were generally raised in individual cities,
towns, and counties.

Contrabands Fugitive slaves.

'Copperhead' A derogatory term for a Peace Democrat which is still used by most
historians.

Corps Following the practise and terminology of Napoleon, for most of the war
the Union and Confederate armies organized two or more divisions into corps; a
corps included infantry, cavalry, and artillery units. In the Union army, a major
general commanded a corps; in the Confederate army a lieutenant general did.

Division A military unit composed of several brigades, commanded by major
generals in the Confederate army and by either a brigadier or a major general in
the Union army. Confederate divisions tended to contain more brigades than
Union divisions.

Dough face A derogatory term for northern politicians viewed as catering to
southern interests; 'a northern man of southern principles.'

Electoral vote The American people do not directly elect the president. Instead, on
a state-by-state basis, they elect members of the electoral college, who then elect

the president. Since a state's electoral vote is distributed not proportionately but under a 'winner-takes-all' rule, there can be considerable divergence between a candidate's popular vote and his electoral vote. For example, in 1864, McClellan won 45 percent of the popular vote but less than 10 percent of the electoral vote.

Feint   In tactics, a deceptive assault that is intended to distract the enemy from the actual assault.

Flank; flank attack   When a military unit deploys into line, its right and left sides are its flanks; an attack on the flank, as compared to the more dangerous attack on the front of the line, is a flank attack.

Free Soil   The political doctrine that United States territories should exclude slavery; also the name of a political party.

Greenbacks   Paper-money that was issued by the Union government in 1862. So-called because one side was printed in green ink.

Haitian Revolution (1791–1804)   Haiti, the western third of the island of Hispaniola, was granted independence from France in 1804 after a long war, largely a slave insurrection, marked by atrocities on both sides. Haiti was the first independent black nation in the Western Hemisphere. For many white Americans, the Haitian Revolution symbolized racial war and black atrocity, particularly murder and rape.

Jim Crow   Racial segregation, named after a character in minstrel shows.

Lower South   The first wave of states that seceded – South Carolina, Georgia, Florida, Alabama, Mississippi, Louisiana, Texas. Cotton was grown outside the lower South, and not all of the lower South was devoted to cotton culture, but in general Cotton South and lower South are used interchangeably.

Manifest destiny   The belief, mostly associated with the Democratic Party, that the United States should and would occupy the whole of the North American continent.

Militia   The military organization of individual states; the president could call upon the states for the use of their militia.

Moral suasion   Moral persuasion. Garrisonian abolitionists tended to reject law itself as a use of force and initially believed the way to end slavery was through convincing slaveholders that slavery was a sin. They referred to this tactic as 'moral suasion.'

Planter   A landholder owning twenty or more slaves.

Popular sovereignty   The political doctrine, espoused by Stephen Douglas, that the people of a territory should determine the presence or absence of slavery in that territory; Douglas left it unclear, however, at what point the people could make that decision.

Raid   As distinct from an invasion, a movement into enemy territory intended not to take and hold territory but to destroy supplies and disrupt the enemy's plans.

Secession   The withdrawal of a state from the United States, based on the belief that each state retained its sovereignty when it entered the Union and that the Constitution was a compact among the states rather than the creation of the American people as a whole.

Trent *affair*   On November 8, 1862, a Union warship stopped and boarded the British mail steamer *Trent* and then seized James M. Mason and John Slidell, two Confederate diplomats. Upon British demand, the United States released the prisoners.

Upcountry   A term used to refer to the Piedmont and mountain areas of the South.

Whigs   In the period of the Second American Party System, the party that formed around opposition to 'King' Andrew Jackson; the party that favored government sponsorship of economic development.

Yeomen   Nonslaveholding farmers.

WHO'S WHO

Adams, Charles Francis, Sr. (1807–86)   During the Civil War, the United States minister to Great Britain.

Anderson, Robert (1805–71)   Career soldier, commanding at Fort Sumter in April 1861. He was promoted to general in May 1861 but retired in 1863.

Anthony, Susan B. (1820–1906)   Abolitionist, feminist, temperance advocate. Along with Elizabeth Cady Stanton, Anthony organized the National Women's Loyal League.

Banks, Nathaniel Preston (1816–94)   Republican politician and Union general; governor of Massachusetts, 1858–61; appointed major general in 1861. He campaigned unsuccessfully against Stonewall Jackson in summer 1861. He was given command of the Department of the Gulf and conducted the successful Port Hudson Campaign and the disastrous Red River Campaign, the latter leading to his removal from command and his resignation. He also oversaw the military occupation and the wartime political Reconstruction of Louisiana. He was a postwar Congressman.

Barton, Clara (1821–1912)   Organizer of relief efforts for Union soldiers, Barton worked at army hospitals unofficially until appointed superintendent of nurses by Benjamin Butler. She founded the American Red Cross in 1881.

Beauregard, Pierre Gustave Toutant (1818–93)   Confederate general. Confederate commander at the attack on Fort Sumter, and appointed full general in August 1861, Beauregard nonetheless is most familiar for campaigns in which he served as second-in-command – Battles of First Bull Run and Shiloh. Because of President Davis's aversion toward him, Beauregard spent much of the war shunted into inactive commands.

Bell, John (1797–1869)   Tennessee Senator; Constitutional Unionist presidential candidate in 1860.

Birney, James G. (1792–1857)   Liberty Party presidential nominee in 1840 and 1844.

Booth, John Wilkes (1838–65)   Actor, Confederate sympathizer, assassin of Lincoln.

Bragg, Braxton (1817–76)   Prewar army officer and planter; Confederate general. Bragg commanded the Army of Tennessee from June 1862 until his resignation following its defeat at Chattanooga in November 1863. As a commander, Bragg was generally able but unpopular.

Breckinridge, John (1821–75)   Vice-President of the United States, 1857–60; presidential candidate; Confederate general; Confederate Secretary of War, 1865. Breckinridge, a Kentuckian, commanded a corps at Shiloh, Stone's River, and Chickamauga. In 1864, he came east and served in the Shenandoah Valley and elsewhere. He was also Davis's last Secretary of War.

Brown, John (1800–59)   Abolitionist, antislavery guerrilla, terrorist. Brown was prominent in the struggle against slavery in prewar Kansas but achieved national fame for his October 1851 attempt to create a slave insurrection at Harper's Ferry, Virginia. This failed insurrection as well as his subsequent trial and execution, escalated tensions between proslavery and antislavery advocates.

Brown, Joseph (1821–94)   Wartime governor of Georgia. Brown's political career began in antebellum Georgia, ran through the war, continued into Reconstruction and far beyond, but he is best known as a vigorous advocate of Georgia's interests and of states rights during the war years, and as an opponent of the Davis administration.

Brownlow, William (1805–77)   Better known as 'Parson Brownlow.' Methodist preacher; Whig journalist; Tennessee Unionist. Because of his opposition to the Confederacy, Brownlow's newspaper was suppressed and he was banished from the Confederacy. He later returned to occupied Tennessee as a newspaper editor and politician. After the war, he served as governor (1865–69) and as a Senator (1869–75).

Buchanan, James (1791–1868)   Democratic President of the United States, 1857–61. Buchanan's presidency was marred by his inability to deal with the slavery issue, and in particular by his collusion with Roger Brook Taney in the Dred Scott decision. He believed secession was unconstitutional but thought federal coercion of a state was unconstitutional as well.

Buell, Don Carlos (1818–98)   Union general. Commanded the Army of the Ohio until the Battle of Perryville (October 8, 1862) after which the army was reorganized into the Army of the Cumberland and Buell was relieved of duty.

Burnside, Ambrose (1824–81)   Union general. Best known as commander of the Army of the Potomac during the Fredericksburg Campaign and the subsequent 'mud march,' Burnside had a broad-ranging career. He helped develop a breech-loading carbine much used by Union cavalry; he became Rhode Island's governor and Senator; he commanded the Roanoke Expedition, the Department of the Ohio, and defense of Knoxville, and an army corps operating in conjunction with the Army of the Potomac during spring 1864.

Butler, Benjamin (1818–93)   Union general and political chameleon. Butler was a prewar Democrat, a Breckinridge supporter in 1860, a major general of volunteers, a Radical Republican Congressman, governor of Massachusetts, and a Greenbacker Congressman and presidential candidate. During the war, his legal and administrative brilliance was matched only by his military ineptitude. He botched his command at Big Bethel, Bermuda Hundred, and Fort Fisher, but his vigorous actions at the war's start helped secure Maryland for the Union. His administration of New Orleans was effective, if corrupt, and his designation of runaway slaves as 'contraband of war' created a legal loophole that help transform Union policy toward slavery.

Chase, Salmon P. (1808–73)   Republican politician and presidential aspirant; wartime Secretary of the Treasury; Justice of the US Supreme Court. Chase, one of the founders of the Republican Party, came to Lincoln's Cabinet convinced of his ability to manipulate Lincoln but came to recognize the president's strength. Nonetheless, Chase maneuvered to replace Lincoln as the Republican nominee in the 1864 election. Subsequently, Lincoln appointed Chase to the Supreme Court.

Cleburne, Patrick (1828–64)   Irish immigrant and Confederate general, Cleburne advocated that slaves be emancipated and recruited into the Confederate army.

Cooke, Jay (1821–1905)   Financier. Cooke, whose family had connections to Salmon P. Chase, Lincoln's Secretary of Treasury, helped raise money for the war effort by marketing government bonds on commission. He also advised the government on other financial matters, particularly the restructuring of banking on the national level.

Crittenden, John J. (1787–1863)   Kentucky Senator. After secession, Crittenden worked for a compromise to reunite the country. After war started, Crittenden advocated policies designed to keep Kentucky and other border states in the Union and found himself increasingly in conflict with the administration and the Republican Party in Congress.

Davis, Henry Winter (1817–65)   Maryland Congressman and Radical Republican, best known for the Wade–Davis bill.

Davis, Jefferson (1808–89)   Confederate president. Prior to the war, Davis served as a Congressman, a colonel in the Mexican War, Secretary of War, and US Senator from Mississippi. Resigning his seat following Mississippi's secession, Davis expected a Confederate military command. Instead, he was elected at first provisional president and later president of the Confederacy. His performance as president drew much criticism at the time and after, but few have been able to suggest a better choice available to the Confederacy.

Dix, Dorethea (1802–87)   Well known as a campaigner for reform of prisons and in the treatment of the mentally ill, during the war Dix was superintendent of women nurses for the Union army.

Douglas, Stephen (1813–61)   Democratic Senator from Illinois; 1860 Democratic presidential candidate. During the 1850s, Douglas was a leading architect of compromise over slavery and its extension into the territories. He was particularly known for espousing popular sovereignty.

Douglass, Frederick (1817?–95)   African-American abolitionist. Born a slave, Douglass escaped to freedom in 1838 and became a leading abolitionist orator and author, editing the newspaper the *North Star* and writing his autobiography, *Narrative of the Life of Frederick Douglass*. During the war, he advocated emancipation; he also helped raise Union soldiers from the northern African-American community.

Early, Jubal (1816–94)   Confederate general. Early was more prominent after the war as a Lost Cause spokesman than he was during his military career, but he served well in the Army of Northern Virginia and achieved an independent command, the Army of the Valley, as well as the rank of lieutenant general (May 1864). The Army of the Valley campaigned successfully against Union General David Hunter's forces and threatened Washington, DC in July 1864, but was ultimately defeated by Phil Sheridan's Army of the Shenandoah in the autumn of that year.

Fremont, John (1813–90)   Union general and politician. In 1861, Fremont commanded the Western Department – essentially St Louis and the state of Missouri. His military failures and his unauthorized emancipation of Missouri slaves led to his dismissal. In 1862, Fremont commanded a small army in Virginia that opposed Stonewall Jackson's forces but achieved no military success; he resigned his command rather than serve under Pope. In 1864, Fremont, who had been the Republican presidential candidate in 1856, attempted to gain the presidency as the nominee of a third party but was out-maneuvered as thoroughly by Lincoln as he had ever been by Jackson.

Garrison, William Lloyd (1805–79)   Abolitionist. Garrison edited the *Liberator* and organized the American Anti-Slavery Society.

Grant, Ulysses S. (1822–85)   Union general. Grant rose to command the Union army and coordinated Union victory. Early in the war Grant achieved fame by taking Forts Henry and Donelson, but he lost much of his reputation by his near-defeat at Shiloh in April 1862 and he considered resigning from the service. His successful campaign against Vicksburg, Mississippi, however, earned him overall command in the West, and his relief of Chattanooga and defeat of the Confederate Army of Tennessee led to his appointment as general-in-chief. In 1864 and 1865, Grant in effect commanded the Army of the Potomac in the field but while that army engaged Lee's Army of Northern Virginia, Grant's subordinates conducted campaigns in other theaters, including great raids through the Confederate countryside. After the war, Grant became president and the corruption that surrounded his administration once again cost him much of his reputation.

Halleck, Henry (1815–72)   Union general. Halleck, having supervised the successful campaigns of Grant and Buell in the West, was appointed general-in-chief in July 1862, but never actually acted in that role. Instead, he (and Lincoln and Stanton) turned the office into that of a chief-of-staff, an appointment Halleck later held when Grant became general-in-chief.

Holden, William W. (1818–92)   A reluctant secessionist, Holden became the leader of North Carolina's peace movement and ran unsuccessfully for governor. After the war, Andrew Johnson appointed Holden governor; he was also elected governor as a Republican in 1868.

Hood, John Bell (1831–1879)   Confederate general. Hood served under R. E. Lee in the prewar US army and later in the Army of Northern Virginia, where he was a division commander under Longstreet. Wounded at Gettysburg and Chickamauga, Hood was promoted to corps command in the Army of Tennessee under Joseph E. Johnston in February 1864. Hood connived at Johnston's removal and received army command in July 1864. Hood immediately attacked Sherman's forces around Atlanta. After Sherman took that city, Hood moved into Tennessee, hoping to lure Sherman into following him. Instead, Sherman dispatched Thomas and the Army of the Cumberland which defeated the Army of Tennessee at the Battle of Nashville (December 1864). In January 1865, Hood resigned his command.

Hooker, Joseph (1814–79)   Union general. A West Point graduate and a veteran of the Mexican War, Hooker served as both a divisional and corps commander in the Army of the Potomac before receiving overall command. That army's defeat at Chancellorsville (May 1–4, 1863) hurt Hooker's prestige and he later resigned its command. He commanded two corps in the Chattanooga and Atlanta campaigns, but resigned again when Sherman failed to promote him on the death of General James B. McPherson.

Hunter, David (1802–66)   Union general. Hunter is remembered both for his usually unsuccessful military campaigns against Charleston in 1862 and in the Shenandoah Valley in 1864, and his antislavery actions. In 1862, Hunter tried to abolish slavery in the Department of the South only to have Lincoln countermand his orders. He organized one of the first African-American regiments, the First South Carolina.

Jackson, Thomas J. 'Stonewall' (1824–63)   Confederate general. Jackson and his brigade received the nickname 'Stonewall' for coolness under fire at the First Battle of Bull Run. Jackson also received a promotion to command in the Shenandoah Valley, where his campaigns against three uncoordinated Union armies interfered with McClellan's plans for the major Union effort against Richmond. When Lee became commander of the Confederate forces outside Richmond, he ordered Jackson to bring his army to him. Jackson initially performed poorly as Lee's subordinate, but rapidly became a brilliant corps commander whose abilities proved crucial to the Army of Northern Virginia. Jackson died of wounds received at the Battle of Chancellorsville, a loss from which the Army of Northern Virginia never fully recovered.

Johnson, Andrew (1808–75)   Tennessee Unionist; military governor of occupied Tennessee, 1862–65. Johnson, the most prominent southern Unionist and the only Senator from a Confederate state who refused to resign his seat, proved an effective governor of occupied Tennessee. In 1864, the Republicans, running as the Union Party in an effort to broaden their appeal, selected the southern ex-Democrat Johnson as their vice-presidential candidate. Lincoln's assassination made him president at the war's end.

Johnston, Albert Sydney (1803–62)   Confederate general. Johnston, one of the first Confederate full generals, received command of the West and had lost Kentucky and Tennessee by spring of 1862. He died at the Battle of Shiloh, leaving behind an inexplicably good military reputation.

Johnston, Joseph (1807–91)   Confederate general. Johnston was one of the Confederate's highest ranking generals but a battlefield wound, his feuds with the president, and his failure to take responsibility during the Vicksburg Campaign caused him to spend much of the war out of action. He commanded Confederate forces in Virginia until he was wounded at the Battle of Seven Pines. After his recuperation he was given command in the West, but failed to exercise it until he was ordered to take over the Army of Tennessee after Bragg's resignation. Under his command that army retreated brilliantly before Sherman's advance on Atlanta. Davis removed him in July 1864, but was forced to return him to command of what was left of the Army of Tennessee after Hood mishandled it in his Tennessee Campaign.

Lee, Robert Edward (1807–70)   Confederate general. A professional soldier, Lee commanded the Army of Northern Virginia, the most successful Confederate army, from June 1862 till the war's end. In February 1865, Davis appointed Lee general-in-chief of all Confederate armies, but Lee remained with the Army of Northern Virginia and never acted as overall commander. After the war, Lee, who had once been superintendent of the US Military Academy, became president of Washington University.

Lincoln, Abraham (1809–65)   Civil War President of the United States. No president had less political experience than Lincoln; he came to office having served one term in Congress in the 1840s and as a veteran of a vigorous but unsuccessful campaign for the Senate. A former Whig, Lincoln deferred to Congress in matters of domestic policy, but he believed in a strong presidency in issues related to the war and to the Reconstruction of the Union. Furthermore, as a political newcomer, he never entirely gained control over his own party. As for the issues of slavery and emancipation, some argue that Lincoln brilliantly transformed the war for Union into an antislavery crusade as well, while others maintain he provided little real leadership and perhaps even lagged behind northern public opinion. His assassination on Good Friday, 1865 gained him the status of martyr, an apotheosis that surely would have left this most practical man bemused.

Longstreet, James (1821–1904)   Confederate general. A career army officer, Longstreet served as a division commander under Joseph E. Johnston and a corp commander under R. E. Lee and Braxton Bragg. His desire for independent command also led him to the inconsequential Suffolk Campaign (spring 1863) and the ineffective Knoxville Campaign (autumn 1863); after the failure of the last he returned to the Army of Northern Virginia and remained with it until the war's end. A postwar Republican officeholder, he became a favorite whipping-boy of Jubal Early and other Lost Cause spokesmen.

Mason, James (1798–1871) Confederate diplomat. The Confederacy appointed Mason ambassador to Great Britain but he was never received. Nonetheless, he spent the war as the Confederacy's man in London.

McClellan, George (1826–85) Union general and Democratic presidential nominee. After the First Bull Run débâcle, McClellan became commander of the Army of the Potomac and, briefly, general-in-chief of all Union armies. His Peninsula Campaign ended in failure when he retreated in face of a series of frontal assaults made by a numerically inferior enemy. McClellan retained command of the Army of the Potomac but most of its units were transferred to John Pope's Army of Virginia. After Pope's defeat, McClellan regained command of these units and defeated Lee at the Battle of Antietam. Nonetheless, his caution in that campaign and his well-publicized anti-administration views led to his dismissal. McClellan ran against Lincoln for president in 1864.

McPherson, James B. (1828–64) Union general. McPherson commanded a corps in the Army of the Tennessee under Grant and Sherman and was later promoted to its overall command. He was killed in action near Atlanta, July 22, 1864.

Meade, George Gordon (1815–72) Union general. Meade served under the various commanders of the Army of the Potomac until appointed to the post himself in the middle of the Gettysburg Campaign. Meade retained that command until the end of the war, but after spring of 1864, Grant effectively directed the Army of the Potomac.

Meigs, Montgomery (1816–92) Quartermaster general of the Union army.

Morton, Oliver (1823–77) Wartime governor of Indiana. No other governor during the Civil War exercised the authority that Morton did, at one time governing the state with no legislative appropriations. Distrusting the legislature, Morton refused to call it into session and relied instead on loans from the federal government and the private sector as well as profits earned by the state arsenal. Indiana raised and largely maintained 150,000 Union soldiers. After the war, Morton became a Senator and generally supported the so-called Radical Republicans.

Pendleton, George (1825–89) Congressman from Ohio and Democratic vice-presidential candidate. Pendleton, better remembered for sponsoring civil service legislation, was a leading Peace Democrat during the war and in 1864 ran for vice-president – on the same ticket as War Democrat George McClellan.

Phillips, Wendell (1811–84) Abolitionist and noted wartime critic of Lincoln.

Polk, James K. (1795–1849) As president, Polk deliberately provoked a war with Mexico which acquired what is now California, New Mexico, Arizona, Colorado, Nevada, Utah and Wyoming, thereby reopening the debate over the expansion of slavery into federal territories.

Pope, John (1822–92)   Union general. A West Pointer, Pope went from a successful campaign along the Mississippi River to failure in the East. After his defeat at the Second Battle of Bull Run, Pope was sent to the western frontier, where he conducted operations against Native Americans; in effect, he was transferred from one war to another.

Rosecrans, William (1819–98)   Union general. Rosecrans commanded the Army of the Cumberland from its creation in October 1862, through the battle of Stone's River and the successful campaign to take Chattanooga, until its defeat at Chickamauga (September 1863) and the Confederate siege of Chattanooga led to his removal. After the war, Rosecrans held various political offices.

Schofield, John M. (1831–1906)   Union general. Schofield, a career officer, served in various capacities during the war, most notably as Union commander at the Battle of Frankin (November 30, 1864).

Scott, Dred (1795–1858)   Plaintiff in *Dred Scott v. Sanford*. Scott, born a slave, sued for his freedom first in the Missouri courts and then in the federal court, arguing that his residence in a free territory had emancipated him. The Dred Scott Case reached the Supreme Court which decided against the plaintiff in 1856.

Scott, Winfield (1786–1866)   Union general. As the Civil War began, Scott was the commander of the US army, but he soon resigned. His Anaconda Plan, which called for splitting the Confederacy by the conquest of the Mississippi River, may be regarded as the basic blueprint for overall Union strategy.

Seward, William H. (1801–72)   Union Secretary of State. A former governor of New York, a founder of the Republican Party, and a US Senator, Seward entered the cabinet expecting to play prime minister to a figurehead president. Lincoln disappointed him by proving stronger than expected. Seward's policy looked toward keeping European nations from supporting the Confederacy. He succeeded, although the credit more properly belongs to British Prime Minister Palmerston.

Seymour, Horatio (1810–86)   Democratic politician; governor of New York, 1862–64; opponent of Republican war measures, particularly conscription and emancipation, and advocate of states' rights; defeated for re-election in 1864.

Sheridan, Philip H. (1831–88)   Union general. A career officer, Sheridan rose from captain to major general during the war, and eventually became full general and commander of the entire army. Sheridan served with the Army of the Cumberland but when Grant went east to direct the Army of the Potomac, he brought Sheridan along to command that army's cavalry. In August 1864, Grant gave Sheridan command of the Army of the Shenandoah which defeated Jubal Early's Army of the Valley and destroyed the autumn crops. At the Battle of Five Forks (April 1, 1865), Sheridan's troops turned the Confederate flank and put R. E. Lee and the Army of Northern Virginia on the road to Appomattox.

Sherman, William Tecumseh (1820–91)   Union general. A prewar army officer, Sherman served much of the war under U. S. Grant, his fortunes rising as his friend's did. In 1864, when Grant received command of all Union armies, he left Sherman in the West, where Sherman conducted the Atlanta Campaign, the March to the Sea and the Campaign of the Carolinas. After the war, Sherman became general-in-chief of the US army, once again serving under Grant who was by that time president.

Smith, E. Kirby (1824–93) Confederate general, best known for his command of the Trans-Mississippi Department.

Stanton, Edwin (1814–69) Union Secretary of War, 1862–68. Stanton's background was legal not military, but his appointment to Lincoln's Cabinet made him one of the key Union strategic planners and gave vigorous administration to the War Department.

Stanton, Elizabeth Cady (1815–1902) Feminist and abolitionist. Stanton along with Susan B. Anthony, organized the Women's National Loyal League, which petitioned Congress for emancipation. She opposed the Fourteenth and Fifteenth Amendments.

Stephens, Alexander (1812–83) Confederate vice-president and Congressman from Georgia, Stephens initially opposed secession, but accepted the Confederate vice-presidency. He is best remembered as one of Jefferson Davis's principal political adversaries.

Stevens, Thaddeus (1792–1868) Antislavery politician. Elected to Congress in 1848 and remaining there until his death, Stevens was an implacable enemy of slavery. During the Civil War and the postwar period Stevens advocated tough Reconstruction terms, confiscation of rebel property, and civil and political rights for African Americans.

Sumner, Charles (1811–74) Antislavery Senator from Massachusetts, 1851–74. Sumner was a prominent Radical Republican and the Senate leader in the fight for civil rights legislation. He offered the theory of 'state suicide' as justification for sweeping Reconstruction policies.

Taney, Roger Brooke (1777–1864) Democratic politician; Chief Justice of the Supreme Court and author of the Dred Scott decision. Taney's Dred Scott decision, which ruled that any prohibition on slavery in federal territory was unconstitutional, encouraged proslavery extremists.

Thomas, George H. (1816–70) Union general. A Southern Unionist and prewar army officer, Thomas served ably under Halleck, Buell, and Rosecrans. The stand of his corps at Chickamauga earned him the nickname 'the Rock of Chickamauga' and command of the Army of the Cumberland. That army fought under Grant's immediate supervision in the Chattanooga Campaign and under Sherman's in the Atlanta Campaign, but operated more independently during Confederate General Hood's invasion of Tennessee in 1864. Thomas defeated Hood at the Battle of Nashville (December 1864) and subsequently was promoted to major general. At the war's close, he remained in the army until his death in 1870.

Tompkins, Sally (1833–1916)   Hospital administrator. Commissioned as a captain in the Confederate Army, Tompkins ran a remarkably effective hospital in Richmond, Virginia.

Toombs, Robert (1810–85)   Southern politician and Confederate general. As a Senator from Georgia (1852–61), Toombs was a leader in the proslavery, Southern Rights cause. In 1860 and 1861, he advocated Georgia's secession. Toombs expected the Confederacy's presidency but was politically out-man-euvered. He served briefly as the Confederacy's Secretary of State; became, simultaneously, Confederate general and Confederate Congressman. He resigned from the army in 1863. After the war, Toombs remained 'unreconstructed', never accepting a pardon and retiring from public life.

Van Buren, Martin (1782–1862)   Ex-president and one of the principal architects of the Democratic Party, he ran for the presidency on the Free Soil ticket in 1848, but returned to the Democratic Party.

Vance, Zebulan (1830–94)   Confederate colonel; governor of North Carolina, 1862–65. After the war, he served as governor again (1876–78) and as Senator (1879–94).

Wade, Benjamin (1800–78)   Republican politician. First a Whig, then a Republi-can, Wade served as US Senator from Ohio for three terms. Wade advocated tougher Reconstruction terms than did Lincoln and was one of the authors of the Wade–Davis bill (1864) that sought to overturn presidential Reconstruction.

Whitman, Walt (1819–92)   Poet. Whitman volunteered as a nurse during the war; the poems in *Drum-Taps* consider the Civil War experience, in particular the assassination of Lincoln.

Wilmot, David (1814–68)   Pennsylvania politician. In 1846, Wilmot, a Democratic representative to Congress, added a proviso to a bill funding the Mexican War that forbade slavery from expanding into any territory acquired by the war. Wilmot later joined the Free Soil and Republican parties.

Wirz, Henry (1823–65)   Wirz, commandant of the prisoner-of-war camp outside of Andersonville, Georgia, was one of the few Confederates executed after the war.

BIBLIOGRAPHY

FURTHER READING

The most important set of published primary sources for military aspects of the war is the 128-volume *The War of the Rebellion: A Compilation of the Official Records of the Union and Confederate Armies* (Washington, DC, 1880–1901). A selection of federal government records concerning emancipation and the freed people is being made available in Ira Berlin et al., *Freedom: A Documentary History of Emancipation, 1861–1867* (Cambridge and New York: Cambridge University Press, 1982–). Politics can be considered from the points of view of both the Confederate and United State presidents in their papers: Haskell Monroe, et al., eds, *The Papers of Jefferson Davis* (Baton Rouge, LA and London: Louisiana State University Press, 1971–) and Roy P. Başlor, ed., *The Collected Works of Abraham Lincoln* (New Brunswick, NJ: Rutgers University Press, 1953)

James M. McPherson has written the best recent synthetic overviews of the war era in his *Ordeal by Fire* (New York: Alfred A. Knopf, 1982) and *Battle Cry of Freedom* (New York and Oxford: Oxford University Press, 1988). Shelby Foote's much-admired *The Civil War* (New York: Random House, 1963–74) is a masterpiece of narrative but a pedestrian interpretation. The most significant twentieth-century interpretation of the Civil War overall is found in the relevant four volumes of Allen Nevin's *Ordeal of the Union* (New York: Scribner, 1959–71), the influence of which can be seen in nearly every textbook on the war since its publication. Two major interpretations of the period written by British historians are Peter J. Parish, *The American Civil War* (London: Eyre Methuen, 1975) and William R. Brock, *Conflict and Transformation: The United States, 1844–1877* (Harmondsworth, England: Penguin, 1973).

The coming of the war is deftly treated in Brian Holden Reid, *The Origins of the American Civil War* (London: Longman, 1996). David M. Potter, *The Impending Crisis: 1848–1861* (New York: Harper & Row, 1976) remains the finest account of the politics of sectional conflict.

The best military history of the war is Herman Hattaway and Archer Jones, *How the North Won* (Urbana, IL: University of Illinois Press, 1991), the publication of which immediately rendered old-fashioned and out-of-date many predominantly military histories of the war, including some that had not yet been written. Hattaway and Jones demonstrate how narrative can be combined with military analysis. Jones's later *Civil War Command and Strategy* (New York: The Free Press, 1992) is also useful, particularly for exploding old myths. Howard Jones, *The Union in Peril* (Chapel Hill, NC: University of North Carolina Press, 1992) does the same for many misconceptions in diplomatic history.

Phillip Shaw Paludan's *A People's Contest* (New York: Harper & Row, 1988) is that rarity in a work of synthesis – a book that raises as many questions as it answers. Nobody has gone as far as Paludan in integrating social and economic history with the traditional studies of the Civil War. *A People's Contest* is an important book for all students of American history. J. Matthew Gallman's *The North Fights the Civil War: The Home Front* (Chicago, IL: Ivan Dee, 1994) is another fine social history of the war, one which explicitly contrasts the northern and southern experience. As both of these studies make clear, much more needs to be done on the social and economic history of the wartime North. Richard Franklin Benzel, *Yankee Leviathan: The Origins of Central State Authority in America, 1859–1877* (Cambridge: Cambridge University Press, 1990) is the most significant study of the Civil War's relation to the formation of the American state. Maris A. Vinovskis, ed., *Toward a Social History of the American Civil War: Exploratory Essays* (Cambridge: Cambridge University Press, 1990) deals with various issues in social history. An introduction to gender history of the period, North and South, is provided by Catherine Clinton and Nina Silber, eds, *Divided Houses: Gender and the Civil War* (New York: Oxford University Press, 1992).

Northern politics from the point of view of the opposition are studied in Joel H. Silbey's indispensable *A Respectable Minority: The Democratic Party in the Civil War Era, 1860–1868* (New York: Norton, 1977). My discussion of the election of 1864 follows the argument made by William W. Freehling in his essay, 'The Divided South, the Causes of Confederate Defeat, and the Reintegration of Narrative History', in his *The Reintegration of American History: Slavery and the Civil War* (New York: Oxford University Press, 1994).

There is no study of the South during the war that is comparable to Paludan's and Gallman's on the North. Emory Thomas's provocative *The Confederate Nation* (New York: Harper & Row, 1979) and Paul Escott's *After Secession* (Baton Rouge, LA: Louisiana State University Press, 1978) are easily the best books on the subject. Readers intrigued by Thomas's argument will want to read his earlier book, *The Confederacy as Revolutionary Experience* (Englewood Cliffs, NJ: Prentice-Hall, 1971), in which that argument is laid out more starkly. George C. Rable's *The Confederate Republic* (Chapel Hill, NC: University of North Carolina Press, 1994) is an important study of Confederate politics, and William C. Davis's *'A Government of Our Own'* (New York: The Free Press, 1994) describes the creation of the Confederate government. Richard E. Beringer, Herman Hattaway, Archer Jones and William N. Still, Jr., *Why the South Lost the Civil War* (Athens, GA: University of Georgia Press, 1987) is the most thorough argument that internal factors explain Confederate defeat; perhaps the most overstated as well. A reply can be found in Gary W. Gallagher, *The Confederate War* (Cambridge, MA: Harvard University Press, 1997).

An early and essential social history of the Confederacy is Bell Irvin Wiley, *The Plain People of the Confederacy* (Baton Rouge, LA: Louisiana State University Press, 1943). Excellent community studies include Daniel W. Crofts, *Old Southampton: Politics and Society in a Virginia County, 1834–1869* (Charlottesville, VA: University Press of Virginia, 1992) and Robert C. Kenzer, *Kinship and Neighborhood in a Southern Community: Orange County, North Carolina, 1849–1881* (Knoxville, TN: University of Tennessee Press, 1987). An overview of the occupied South is Stephen V. Ash, *When the Yankees Came: Conflict and Chaos in the Occupied South, 1861–1865* (Chapel Hill, NC: University of North Carolina Press, 1995).

The essential study on emancipation and the southern black experience is the previously cited Ira Berlin, et al., eds, *Freedom: A Documentary History of*

Emancipation, 1861–1867. In particular, I relied heavily on their *Slaves No More* (Cambridge: Cambridge University Press, 1992) for my discussion of emancipation. Wartime Reconstruction is considered in Eric Foner, *Reconstruction: America's Unfinished Revolution* (New York: Harper & Row, 1988) and Peyton McCrary, *Abraham Lincoln and Reconstruction: The Louisiana Experiment* (Princeton, NJ: Princeton University Press, 1978). The emergence of a new labor system in the post-emancipation South is discussed in Clarence L. Mohr, *On the Threshold of Freedom: Masters and Slaves in Civil War Georgia* (Athens, GA: University of Georgia Press, 1986), Gerald David Jaynes, *Branches without Roots: Genesis of the Black Working Class in the American South, 1862–1882* (New York: Oxford University Press, 1986), Joseph P. Reidy, *From Slavery to Agrarian Capitalism in the Cotton Plantation South: Central Georgia, 1800–1880* (Chapel Hill, NC: University of North Carolina Press, 1992), Michael Wayne, *The Reshaping of Plantation Society: The Natchez District, 1860–80* (Baton Rouge, LA: Louisiana State University Press, 1983), Willie Lee Rose, *Rehearsal for Reconstruction: The Port Royal Experiment* (New York: Vintage Books, 1967), and Lawrence Powell, *New Masters: Northern Planters during the Civil War and Reconstruction* (New Haven, CT and London: Yale University Press, 1980).

Finally, James McPherson and William Cooper, eds, *Writing the Civil War* (Columbia, SC: University of South Carolina Press, 1998) is the most recent historiographic survey and will guide readers in further reading.

SECONDARY SOURCES

1 Aaron, Daniel, *The Unwritten War: American Writers and the Civil War*. New York: Alfred A. Knopf, 1973.

2 Ash, Stephen V., *When the Yankees Came: Conflict and Chaos in the Occupied South, 1861–1865*. Chapel Hill, NC: University of North Carolina Press, 1995.

3 Benzel, Richard Franklin, *Yankee Leviathan: The Origins of Central State Authority in America, 1859–1877*. Cambridge and New York: Cambridge University Press, 1990.

4 Cashin, Joan E., *Our Common Affairs: Texts from Women in the Old South*. Baltimore, MD: Johns Hopkins University Press, 1996.

5 Cooper, William J., Jr., *The South and the Politics of Slavery*. Baton Rouge, LA: Louisiana State University Press, 1980.

6 Davis, David Brion, *The Problem of Slavery in Western Civilization*. New York and Oxford: Oxford University Press, 1988.

7 Escott, Paul D., *After Secession: Jefferson Davis and the Failure of Confederate Nationalism*. Baton Rouge, LA: Louisiana State University Press, 1978.

8 Faust, Drew Gilpin, *Mothers of Invention: Women of the Slaveholding South in the American Civil War*. Chapel Hill, NC: University of North Carolina Press, 1996.

9 Foner, Eric, *Reconstruction: America's Unfinished Revolution, 1863–1877*. New York: Harper & Row, 1988.

10 Foote, Shelby, *The Civil War: A Narrative* (3 vols). New York: Random House, 1963–74.

11   Fredrickson, George M., *The Inner Civil War: Northern Intellectuals and the Crisis of the Union*. New York: Harper & Row, 1965.

12   Griffith, Paddy, *Battle Tactics of the Civil War*. New Haven, CT and London: Yale University Press, 1989.

13   Hattaway, Herman, and Jones, Archer, *How the North Won: A Military History of the Civil War*. Urbana, IL: University of Illinois Press, 1991.

14   Jones, Archer, *Civil War Command and Strategy: The Process of Victory and Defeat*. New York: The Free Press, 1992.

15   Jones, Howard, *Union in Peril: The Crisis over British Intervention in the Civil War*. Chapel Hill, NC: University of North Carolina Press, 1992.

16   Kenzer, Robert C., *Kinship and Neighborhood in a Southern Community: Orange County, North Carolina, 1849–1881*. Knoxville, TN: University of Tennessee Press, 1987.

17   McPherson, James M., *Ordeal by Fire: The Civil War and Reconstruction*. New York: Alfred A. Knopf, 1982.

18   Millet, Allan R., and Maslowski, Peter, *For the Common Defense: A Military History of the United States of America (Revised and Expanded)*. New York: The Free Press, 1994, pp. 163–247.

19   Mitchell, Reid, 'The Creation of Confederate Loyalties', in Robert H. Abzug and Stephen E. Maizlish, eds, *New Perspectives on Race and Slavery in America: Essays in Honor of Kenneth M. Stampp*. Lexington, KY: University Press of Kentucky, 1986, pp. 93–108.

20   Moore, Barington, *Social Origins of Dictatorship and Democracy: Lord and Peasant in the Making of the Modern World*. Boston, MA: Beacon Press, 1966, pp. 111–59.

21   Owsley, Frank Lawrence, *State Rights in the Confederacy*. Chicago, IL: University of Chicago Press, 1925.

22   Potter, David M., *The Impending Crisis: 1848–1861*. New York: Harper & Row, 1976.

23   Powell, Lawrence N., and Wayne, Michael S., 'Self-interest and the Decline of Confederate Nationalism', in Harry P. Owens and James J. Cooke, eds, *The Old South in the Crucible of War*. Jackson, MS: University Press of Mississippi, 1983, pp. 29–45.

24   Powell, Lawrence, *New Masters: Northern Planters during the Civil War and Reconstruction*. New Haven, CT and London: Yale University Press, 1980.

25   Rable, George C., *Civil Wars: Women and the Crisis of Southern Nationality*. Urbana and Chicago, IL: University of Illinois Press, 1989.

26   Reidy, Joseph P., *From Slavery to Agrarian Capitalism in the Cotton Plantation South: Central Georgia, 1800–1880*. Chapel Hill, NC: University of North Carolina Press, 1992.

27   Rose, Willie Lee, *Rehearsal for Reconstruction: The Port Royal Experiment*. New York: Vintage Books, 1967.

28   Royster, Charles, *The Destructive War: William Tecumseh Sherman, Stonewall Jackson, and the Americans*. New York: Alfred A. Knopf, 1991.

29   Sherman, W. T., *Memoirs of William T. Sherman*. Bloomington, IN: Indiana University Press, 1957.

30   Snay, Mitchell, *Gospel of Disunion: Religion and Separatism in the Antebellum South*. Cambridge and New York: Cambridge University Press, 1993.

31   Stampp, Kenneth M., *The Southern Road to Appomattox*. El Paso, TX: University of Texas at El Paso, 1969.

32   Stampp, Kenneth M., *The Imperilled Union: Essays on the Background of the Civil War*. New York and Oxford: Oxford University Press, 1981.

33   Thomas, Emory M., *The Confederacy as Revolutionary Experience*. Englewood Cliffs, NJ: Prentice-Hall, 1971.

34   Thomas, Emory M., *The Confederate Nation: 1861–1865*. New York: Harper & Row, 1979.

35   Warren, Robert Penn, *The Legacy of the Civil War: Meditations on the Centennial*. New York: Vintage Books, 1864.

36   Wayne, Michael, *The Reshaping of Plantation Society: The Natchez District, 1860–80*. Baton Rouge, LA: Louisiana State University Press, 1983.

37   Wright, Gavin, *Old South, New South: Revolutions in the Southern Economy since the Civil War*. New York: Basic Books, 1986.

38   Yeatman, James E., *A Report on the Condition of the Freedmen of the Mississippi, presented to the Western Sanitary Commission. December 17, 1863, By James E. Yeatman, President of the Commission*. St Louis, 1864.

INDEX

Page numbers in bold refer to biographical details at back of book

weapons, 19–20, 22
Western Sanitary Commission, 36
Whigs, 11, 30–2, 114
Whitman, Walt, 35, 93–4, **124**
Wilderness, Battle of the (1864), 58–9, 110
Wilmot, David, 10, **124**
Wilson, James Harrison, 67
Wirz, Captain Henry, 69, **124**
Woman's National Loyal League, 36, 123
women, 99–100
    Confederacy and white, 49–50

employment of during war, 34, 36, 50
impact of war on status of in North, 36
suffrage movement in North, 36
and volunteerism during war, 35–6
Wright, Gavin, 47
writers, 35

Yeatman, James E., 75
yeomen, 47–8
YMCA, 35

SEMINAR STUDIES IN HISTORY

General Editors: Clive Emsley & Gordon Martel

The series was founded by Patrick Richardson in 1966. Between 1980 and 1996 Roger Lockyer edited the series before handing over to Clive Emsley (Professor of History at the Open University) and Gordon Martel (Professor of International History at the University of Northern British Columbia, Canada and Senior Research Fellow at De Montfort University).

STUART BRITAIN

Social Change and Continuity: England 1550–1750 (Second edition)
Barry Coward   0 582 29442 8

James I (Second edition)
S J Houston   0 582 20911 0

The English Civil War 1640–1649
Martyn Bennett   0 582 35392 0

Charles I, 1625–1640
Brian Quintrell   0 582 00354 7

The English Republic 1649–1660 (Second edition)
Toby Barnard   0 582 08003 7

Radical Puritans in England 1550–1660
R J Acheson   0 582 35515 X

The Restoration and the England of Charles II (Second edition)
John Miller   0 582 29223 9

The Glorious Revolution (Second edition)
John Miller   0 582 29222 0

EARLY MODERN EUROPE

The Renaissance (Second edition)
Alison Brown   0 582 30781 3

The Emperor Charles V
Martyn Rady   0 582 35475 7

French Renaissance Monarchy: Francis I and Henry II (Second edition)
Robert Knecht   0 582 28707 3

The Protestant Reformation in Europe
Andrew Johnston   0 582 07020 1

The French Wars of Religion 1559–1598 (Second edition)
Robert Knecht   0 582 28533 X

Phillip II
Geoffrey Woodward   0 582 07232 8

The Thirty Years' War
Peter Limm   0 582 35373 4

Louis XIV
Peter Campbell   0 582 01770 X

Spain in the Seventeenth Century
Graham Darby   0 582 07234 4

Peter the Great
William Marshall   0 582 00355 5

EUROPE 1789–1918

Britain and the French Revolution
Clive Emsley   0 582 36961 4

Revolution and Terror in France 1789–1795 (Second edition)
D G Wright   0 582 00379 2

Napoleon and Europe
D G Wright   0 582 35457 9

Nineteenth-Century Russia: Opposition to Autocracy
Derek Offord   0 582 35767 5

The Constitutional Monarchy in France 1814–48
Pamela Pilbeam   0 582 31210 8

The 1848 Revolutions (Second edition)
Peter Jones   0 582 06106 7

The Italian Risorgimento
M Clark   0 582 00353 9

Bismark & Germany 1862–1890 (Second edition)
D G Williamson   0 582 29321 9

Imperial Germany 1890–1918
Ian Porter, Ian Armour and Roger Lockyer   0 582 03496 5

The Dissolution of the Austro-Hungarian Empire 1867–1918 (Second edition)
John W Mason   0 582 29466 5

Second Empire and Commune: France 1848–1871 (Second edition)
William H C Smith   0 582 28705 7

France 1870–1914 (Second edition)
Robert Gildea   0 582 29221 2

The Scramble for Africa (Second edition)
M E Chamberlain   0 582 36881 2

Late Imperial Russia 1890–1917
John F Hutchinson   0 582 32721 0

The First World War
Stuart Robson   0 582 31556 5

EUROPE SINCE 1918

The Russian Revolution (Second edition)
Anthony Wood   0 582 35559 1

Lenin's Revolution: Russia, 1917–1921
David Marples   0 582 31917 X

Stalin and Stalinism (Second edition)
Martin McCauley   0 582 27658 6

The Weimar Republic (Second edition) *John Hiden*	0 582 28706 5
The Inter-War Crisis 1919–1939 *Richard Overy*	0 582 35379 3
Fascism and the Right in Europe, 1919–1945 *Martin Blinkhorn*	0 582 07021 X
Spain's Civil War (Second edition) *Harry Browne*	0 582 28988 2
The Third Reich (Second edition) *D G Williamson*	0 582 20914 5
The Origins of the Second World War (Second edition) *R J Overy*	0 582 29085 6
The Second World War in Europe *Paul MacKenzie*	0 582 32692 3
Anti-Semitism before the Holocaust *Albert S Lindemann*	0 582 36964 9
The Holocaust: The Third Reich and the Jews *David Engel*	0 582 32720 2
Germany from Defeat to Partition, 1945–1963 *D G Williamson*	0 582 29218 2
Britain and Europe since 1945 *Alex May*	0 582 30778 3
Eastern Europe 1945–1969: From Stalinism to Stagnation *Ben Fowkes*	0 582 32693 1
The Khrushchev Era, 1953–1964 *Martin McCauley*	0 582 27776 0

NINETEENTH-CENTURY BRITAIN

Britain before the Reform Acts: Politics and Society 1815–1832 *Eric J Evans*	0 582 00265 6
Parliamentary Reform in Britain c. 1770–1918 *Eric J Evans*	0 582 29467 3
Democracy and Reform 1815–1885 *D G Wright*	0 582 31400 3
Poverty and Poor Law Reform in Nineteenth-Century Britain, 1834–1914: From Chadwick to Booth *David Englander*	0 582 31554 9
The Birth of Industrial Britain: Economic Change, 1750–1850 *Kenneth Morgan*	0 582 29833 4
Chartism (Third edition) *Edward Royle*	0 582 29080 5

Peel and the Conservative Party 1830–1850
Paul Adelman   0 582 35557 5

Gladstone, Disraeli and later Victorian Politics (Third edition)
Paul Adelman   0 582 29322 7

Britain and Ireland: From Home Rule to Independence
Jeremy Smith   0 582 30193 9

TWENTIETH-CENTURY BRITAIN

The Rise of the Labour Party 1880–1945 (Third edition)
Paul Adelman   0 582 29210 7

The Conservative Party and British Politics 1902–1951
Stuart Ball   0 582 08002 9

The Decline of the Liberal Party 1910–1931 (Second edition)
Paul Adelman   0 582 27733 7

The British Women's Suffrage Campaign 1866–1928
Harold L Smith   0 582 29811 3

War & Society in Britain 1899–1948
Rex Pope   0 582 03531 7

The British Economy since 1914: A Study in Decline?
Rex Pope   0 582 30194 7

Unemployment in Britain between the Wars
Stephen Constantine   0 582 35232 0

The Attlee Governments 1945–1951
Kevin Jefferys   0 582 06105 9

The Conservative Governments 1951–1964
Andrew Boxer   0 582 20913 7

Britain under Thatcher
Anthony Seldon and Daniel Collings   0 582 31714 2

INTERNATIONAL HISTORY

The Eastern Question 1774–1923 (Second edition)
A L Macfie   0 582 29195 X

The Origins of the First World War (Second edition)
Gordon Martel   0 582 28697 2

The United States and the First World War
Jennifer D Keene   0 582 35620 2

Anti-Semitism before the Holocaust
Albert S Lindemann   0 582 36964 9

The Origins of the Cold War, 1941–1949 (Second edition)
Martin McCauley   0 582 27659 4

Russia, America and the Cold War, 1949–1991
Martin McCauley   0 582 27936 4

The Arab–Israeli Conflict
Kirsten E Schulze   0 582 31646 4

The United Nations since 1945: Peacekeeping and the Cold War
Norrie MacQueen   0 582 35673 3

Decolonisation: The British Experience since 1945
Nicholas J White   0 582 29087 2

The Vietnam War
Mitchell Hall   0 582 32859 4

WORLD HISTORY

China in Transformation, 1900–1949
Colin Mackerras   0 582 31209 4

Japan in Transformation, 1952–2000
Jeff Kingston   0 582 41875 5

US HISTORY

America in the Progressive Era, 1890–1914
Lewis L Gould   0 582 35671 7

The United States and the First World War
Jennifer D Keene   0 582 35620 2

The Truman Years, 1945–1953
Mark S Byrnes   0 582 32904 3

The Vietnam War
Mitchell Hall   0 582 32859 4

American Abolitionists
Stanley Harrold   0 582 35738 1

The American Civil War, 1861–1865
Reid Mitchell   0 582 31973 0